Belinda Thomson
studied Gauguin and Symbolism at
the Courtauld Institute of Art, London, and has published
articles and reviews on nineteenth-century French art and
the Nabis group. She is the author of *The Post-Impressionists*, and is currently writing a book
on Vuillard.

WORLD OF ART

This famous series
provides the widest available
range of illustrated books on art in all its aspects.
If you would like to receive a complete list
of titles in print please write to:
THAMES AND HUDSON
30 Bloomsbury Street, London WC1B 3QP
In the United States please write to:
THAMES AND HUDSON INC.
500 Fifth Avenue, New York, New York 10110

1 *Autoportrait au chapeau* 1893

BELINDA THOMSON

GAUGUIN

182 illustrations, 31 in color

THAMES AND HUDSON

For Richard

ACKNOWLEDGMENTS

*I should like to thank the staff of the following museums, art
galleries and libraries for facilitating my research for this book:
Department of Prints and Drawings, The British Museum,
London; Musée Fabre, Montpellier; Cabinet des Dessins,
Musée de Louvre, Paris; Museum of Fine Arts, Boston; Fogg
Art Museum, Cambridge, Mass.; John Rylands Library,
Deansgate, Manchester; Manchester Polytechnic Art Library;
The Open University Library; Witt Library, London. I am
grateful to many other scholars of the period, in particular to
those who have answered queries and provided help: Janine
Bailly-Herzberg; Richard Brettell; Gloria Groom; Christopher
Lloyd; Barbara Schapiro. A debt of thanks also goes to my
family, to my parents and parents-in-law for enabling the
research to be done and, last but not least, to my husband, for
sharing ideas and discoveries, reading the manuscript with a
critical eye and offering unstinting encouragement.*

Contents

2 *Gauguin devant son chevalet* 1885

Paul Gauguin made it his business to achieve a high public profile during his lifetime and was one of the first independent artists of his generation to gain international recognition. But his prominence has probably always had as much to do with the dramatic events of his life as with the appeal of his art. Gauguin's flight from European civilization to take up a primitive existence in Tahiti became legendary; indeed, it did much to fuel the myth of the artist as tortured soul, destined to be misunderstood and to live outside the bounds of civilized society. Gauguin himself was well aware of the advantage such personal notoriety could have for his work. It did not much seem to matter that his behaviour and character were censured rather than praised; the important thing was to be talked about.

'Where does the execution of a picture begin and where does it end?' Gauguin was prompted to ask this question about his own monumental canvas *D'Où venons-nous? Que sommes-nous? Où allons-nous?* of 1897. In a sense, it is a question that dominates this book. Few artists have been so unwilling as he was to allow their works to take their chances in the world, or been so keen to control the ways in which they were understood. In many instances, Gauguin's creative influence continued, in the form of changes to a title or authoritative written exegeses, long after a work had left his studio and he often intervened in the equally important stage of public reception and critical interpretation. I have taken the view that the words surrounding his works of art are as vital to our understanding of Gauguin as the works themselves; only by attending to them both can we hope to evaluate the meaning and importance he wanted to have and could have had for his own time.

For the historian, Gauguin's unfortunate knack of making enemies of formerly faithful friends and admirers means that the copious documentation surrounding his life's work is more than usually riddled with misrepresentations and half-truths, and needs to be sifted carefully. Indeed, his life and work are full of contradictions. He had

160

7

been a devoted husband and father but scarcely saw his wife and children for the last eighteen years of his life. He had been a wealthy stockbroker and patron of the arts but then chose the impoverished existence of an artist at the mercy of the buyer's whim. A profound admirer of the classical tradition, he turned primitive, uprooting himself from his cultural origins and exiling himself from his contemporaries and public on a remote South Sea island. The explanation for this series of paradoxes and self-denials does not lie with Gauguin alone. It has as much to do with the complex set of circumstances in which he and all other artists of the late nineteenth century found themselves, as soon as they attempted to work outside the limitations imposed by the institutions and academic conventions of their day. But Gauguin promoted the notion that within him, and outside his control, two diametrically opposed natures co-existed, the sensitive man and the savage. If the former side was to the fore in his early years, later on it was his savage nature that enabled him to forge ahead on his chosen primitive path, hardening him against emotional and material sacrifices. He was fond of quoting Degas, who, prompted by seeing the first collection of brilliantly coloured paintings and strangely barbarous carvings Gauguin brought back from Tahiti in 1893, likened him to the 'loup maigre' of La Fontaine's fable, the wolf who is prepared to starve rather than suffer the indignity of a collar and chain. It was a powerful image, but it distorted the realities of Gauguin's existence and as an explanation for his character and motivation is seriously deficient.

Any assessment of Gauguin's contribution to the history of art needs to account for the divergence of views expressed by his contemporaries. On the one hand, artists such as Monet, Pissarro, Cézanne and Signac looked on Gauguin with suspicion, variously dismissing him as a charlatan, opportunist and plagiarist; on the other, artists such as Degas, Maillol and Maurice Denis, not to mention a whole range of lesser-known disciples, including the so-called Pont-Aven group, admired Gauguin's work wholeheartedly, hailing him as the initiator of a formal and decorative revolution. Indeed, almost before Gauguin's death the first signs of that revolution were making themselves evident in the work of the rising avant-garde grouped round Matisse, while the renovation of classicism, signs of which had been detected in Gauguin's later work, became a reality between the two world wars. In the 1980s, when the depiction of the human figure

3 *Pastorales Tahitiennes* 1892

is once again a pressing concern of contemporary artists, and when the ways in which meanings are encoded through signs and cross-cultural symbols are being explored, it is appropriate that the work of Gauguin should again come under scrutiny. He may well prove to have new lessons to teach, beyond the liberation of form and colour from obedience to nature that has been judged by modernist critics as his most important legacy to the twentieth century. But in investigating, from our own standpoint, the significance of Gauguin's art and life, we should never lose sight of the particular and limiting historical factors that determined his ways of seeing.

4 *Mette Gauguin en robe de soir* 1884

CHAPTER ONE

The Part-Time Painter (1848–1884)

When in 1873 Mette Gad, a young Danish woman 'sans profession', married Paul Gauguin, a stockbroker's junior in Paris, she knew nothing of his artistic leanings. So, at least, she was to claim in later years. As far as she was aware, she was marrying an independent man of twenty-five who had spent five years at sea in the merchant navy and now looked set on a promising career in finance. The wedding was a quiet affair in the town hall of the ninth arrondissement, followed by a blessing in the Lutheran church to which Mette, as a Dane, owed allegiance. No members of either family appear to have been present, both parents of Paul Gauguin having died, and the bride's mother deciding to remain in her native Copenhagen. Instead, the witnesses were Gauguin's employer M Bertin, a secretary from the Danish consulate, Gauguin's legal guardian Gustave Arosa, and the latter's aged father. It was probably the Arosas who offered hospitality to the newly-weds, much as they had provided the introduction and social setting for their courtship.

Cultured and comfortably off, Gustave Arosa was a successful stockbroker who had built up a substantial art collection of recent and contemporary paintings, including works by Delacroix, Corot, Courbet and Pissarro. His house in the rue Bréda drew together a varied circle of artistic figures. Whether Mette had really gained no inkling of her future husband's interest in this collection, nor of his own amateur attempts at drawing and painting, seems doubtful. In any event, she was probably warned that she was taking quite a risk in marrying a foreigner of whose family and background she knew so little. A francophile and linguist who greatly enjoyed the life of Paris, Mette Gad had a character as strong and independent as Paul Gauguin's, and it seems likely that at the age of twenty-three she saw this marriage as a way of breaking out of the confines of her bourgeois Danish upbringing.

From letters written to Mette in 1873 by Marie Heegaard, her close friend and travelling companion, Paul Gauguin emerges as a sociable, amusing and eligible catch, somewhat lacking in social graces, but evidently making efforts to overcome his uncouthness. Some years later, however, with less amusement, Mette described him as 'mal élevé', badly brought up, a failing she was by then anxious to avoid reproducing in her own children.

Gauguin's childhood, and that of his mother before him, would nowadays count as 'disturbed'. He had never known the security of family life or a stable home, even from his earliest years, for his father, Clovis Gauguin, a republican journalist, died on board ship while taking his young family into political exile in South America. Paul Gauguin, born in 1848, was just two when they reached Peru and he spent four years there, with his mother and sister, under the protection of distant relatives. By the time he was seven, he and his family were living back in France, under the wing of a bachelor uncle. Gauguin attended schools in Orléans, boarding at a Jesuit seminary until he was fourteen, and then a pre-naval college in Paris. He was given a sound education with a strong emphasis on the classics and literature, a love of which was to manifest itself in his work both as an artist and a writer. Gauguin later remembered his brief childhood spell in Peru as a brilliantly colourful, haunting paradise. But the uncertainty of his mother's social and financial position, the need to gain acceptance from strangers and the experience of two lengthy sea voyages before Gauguin was seven were not promising foundations for a later life of solid bourgeois domesticity.

Aline Gauguin, née Chazal, Gauguin's mother, despite later considering commerce beneath her son, was forced to earn their keep by dressmaking in Paris. (She was fondly commemorated by her son in at least two paintings.) She had spent much of her youth in boarding schools, away from her own ill-matched parents who were separated and at loggerheads. Her mother, Flora Tristan, in whose care she ostensibly was until 1844, was too busy making her fortune as adventuress, and then her reputation as political activist, to provide a home for her daughter. A strange and lonely upbringing it must have been for Aline, to be fought over in successive legal battles and, in 1838, to see her father André Chazal, to all intents and purposes a mild-mannered printmaker, imprisoned for twenty years on an unproven and dubious charge of attempting to murder his wife. If Paul Gauguin knew that his maternal grandfather, from whom he may have inherited his artistic leanings, had served time from 1839 to

5 *La Mère de l'artiste* 1889

1855, and the reason for it, one wonders what effect the knowledge had on him. Certainly he never mentioned it in his copious autobiographical writings, though he clearly found his maternal grandmother, whom he described as an 'anarchist blue-stocking' who 'probably didn't know how to cook', an intriguing figure; one suspects he admired her unconventional style of life, her preparedness to follow the course in which she believed rather than simply obeying the demands of family and society. More doubtful is how far he shared her political views, her historically precocious feminism and her passionate championing of the cause of the workers. Although Gauguin was by choice and family tradition a republican, it may be that the experience of a privileged, almost aristocratic, life in Peru, followed by the usual difficulties of gaining acceptance as an artist, led him later, albeit with tongue in cheek, to hanker after an absolutist régime, a patriarchal society, in which the artist was protected, instead of the democratic system in which talent was fatally neglected.

Gauguin was sufficiently attached to the memory of his parents to name two of his children after them: Aline, his only and much-loved daughter, born in 1877, and Clovis, his second son, born in 1879. Yet his relations with his mother seem to have been somewhat stormy. She died in 1867 and in her will named Gustave Arosa as guardian of her two children, stated her desires concerning the education of her daugher Marie, and effectively washed her hands of her son's future: 'He'll have to make his own way, for he has shown himself so little able to endear himself to all my friends that he's going to find himself very much abandoned.' Evidently, Gauguin came to feel that this tough approach had done him no harm, indeed that he had positively benefited from making his own way as a merchant seaman. Once his eldest son Emil reached the age of eighteen, he argued that he should be left to fend for himself, a course that was totally opposed by his wife, who did all in her power to ensure that her eldest son obtained a good position in his chosen career of engineering.

In view of his unusual family history, though it was tempered by the more sober influence of his father's side, perhaps it is misleading to think of Gauguin as a model family man who unexpectedly and inexplicably kicked over the traces of bourgeois life. It would be more accurate to see the brief ten-year period of settled and comfortable family life in Paris, between 1873 and 1883, as marking a hiatus in a life of upheaval, uncertainty and displacement. Gauguin may have been more at home in the company of painters than he had been with high financiers, but he was referred to frequently by artist contemporaries in Paris as an awkward, meddlesome outsider who had never lost the restless, roving outlook of the sailor.

Helped, no doubt, by the influential Arosa, and equipped with the necessary skills to succeed on the stock market, Gauguin rose quickly in the various finance firms that employed him. His succession of jobs, beginning in 1877, is now thought to have been deliberate, however, to gain more time to pursue his growing passion for painting. As well as attending evening life classes at the Académie Colarossi, from the time of his marriage in 1873 Gauguin devoted his Sundays to *plein air* painting rather than to the more conventional gambling or womanizing, as he later ironically reminded his wife. Certainly, he seems to have been painting landscapes with confidence from at least as early as 1873, if the date on the Fitzwilliam Museum's *Paysage* is   7 correct. Like many painters of his generation, he recognized the current strength of the French landscape tradition; his broadly treated views, the Fitzwilliam one possibly a panorama overlooking an estuary, suggest a general awareness of Camille Corot and a more particular understanding of Henri-Joseph Harpignies. Gauguin's *Paysage avec peupliers* (1875) recalls another Barbizon painter, Narcisse   6 Diaz. The acceptance and favourable critical mention of a still unidentified *Paysage* by Gauguin at the Salon of 1876 must have done much to kindle his artistic ambitions and shows how soon he achieved a level of competence within the somewhat conservative conventions of the day.

At about this time, however, Gauguin was becoming aware of the Impressionist group, who were introducing important changes to the landscape genre by their use of a palette exclusively made up of light tones, their freer paint handling and their more informal settings. Gauguin could have seen their works, which were exhibited regularly in Paris from 1874 onwards, and his assured and sizeable suburban landscape *Les Maraîchers de Vaugirard* (*c.* 1879) shows that,   23 although he was still an amateur, he had moved beyond his exploration of standard and acceptable landscape motifs, just as had the Impressionists. He was now set on a course of independent painting that would henceforth lead him to disdain exhibiting at the official Salon.

By 1879 Gauguin had begun to follow his guardian's example of investing in contemporary works of art, partly, no doubt, because he firmly believed they were important and undervalued, and partly because he needed constant access to examples of Impressionism from which to learn. Building on an already developed taste for the naturalistic Barbizon landscape tradition, which was well represented in Arosa's collection, Gauguin primarily offered his patronage to the less commercially successful landscape Impressionists Guillaumin, Cézanne and Pissarro. It has been thought that Gauguin was first introduced to Camille Pissarro at Arosa's house some time in the early 1870s. In any event, by 1879 Gauguin was simultaneously playing the roles of pupil, patron and dealer to Pissarro, receiving some sort of informal instruction in painting from the elder painter, acquiring occasional works himself and looking out for potential buyers among his stock-market acquaintances, thereby supplementing or by-passing the efforts of Pissarro's dealer, Paul Durand-Ruel. Gauguin's income in 1879 seems to have been very comfortable and his future as a collector probably looked rosy. Although of very different temperaments, Gauguin and Pissarro were to maintain this mutually beneficial relationship until artistic and personal disagreements began to drive them apart during 1885 and 1886. Thus if any one person could take the credit for actively encouraging Gauguin's artistic ambitions at the outset it was Pissarro, as Gauguin acknowledged on the eve of his death. Thanks to Pissarro's intervention, Gauguin was invited to participate in the Impressionist group's fourth exhibition in April 1879, and although his submission was too late to get into the catalogue (he figured instead as the owner of three Pissarros), it nevertheless showed a certain unorthodoxy, or perhaps simply a desire to attract attention on the artist's part. He sent in a piece of sculpture, a marble bust of his son Emil.

23   In *Les Maraîchers de Vaugirard*, Gauguin was probably painting the view from his own house as it would have been almost unthinkable to seek out such an unpromising location, with its high horizon, blanked-off horizontal planes and mere glimpses of an unpicturesque roofscape. The authority for tackling just such a view clearly came from the Impressionists, and more specifically from Pissarro, who
8   had been painting similar working landscapes round his home town of Pontoise for a decade. The broken, fussy brushwork was a new feature in Gauguin's search for an appropriate style, though he also used strong, unvariegated and somewhat acid expanses of green, setting them off with smaller areas of complementary orange-red. Seen as a stage in a learning process, it is less a study of light and atmosphere than an attempt to vary his paint handling by a lighter, more flexible touch and to modernize his landscape settings, to address the suburban motif which was coming to be recognized as the hallmark of landscape Impressionism. In other landscapes done at this

6 *Paysage avec peupliers* 1875

7 *Paysage c.* 1873

8 Camille Pissarro *The Côte des Bœufs at L'Hermitage, near Pontoise* 1877

9 *Les Pommiers en fleurs* 1879

10 *Le Jardin, rue Carcel* 1881

period, his preoccupation seems to have been increasingly to capture minute changes of colour, judging from the picture notes he made on a preparatory drawing for a nocturnal landscape of 1881. By trying at this time to attune his eye to Impressionist concerns for the evanescent effect, in *Les Pommiers en fleurs*, for instance, or *Le Jardin, rue Carcel*, Gauguin's compositions, like Pissarro's, began to suffer from a loss of focus, and the paint texture became somewhat dense and cluttered.

9, 10

An awareness of such shared problems no doubt led Gauguin and Pissarro to take a keen interest in the technical progress being made by Cézanne, a long-standing friend of Pissarro. They may all have worked together during the summer of 1881. To judge from the amusing sketch of a picnic made later by Georges (Manzana) Pissarro, Camille's second son, the Pissarro home at Pontoise became something of a landscapists' colony. Armand Guillaumin was another regular visitor and Gauguin and he established good relations that year; indeed, several critics found close similarities between their paintings. At this so-called period of crisis for Impressionism, much discussion focused on the problem of giving unity to a painting's

11

18

11 Georges Manzana Pissarro *An Impressionist Picnic c. 1881*, with (from left) Guillaumin, Pissarro, Gauguin, Cézanne, Mme Cézanne and the young Manzana

surface while retaining the spontaneity of the initial sensation. Hence Gauguin's half-serious suggestion, made in a letter to Pissarro in 1881: 'Has M Césanne [sic] discovered the exact *formula* for a work that would be accepted by everyone? If he should find the recipe for concentrating the full expression of all his sensations into a single and unique procedure, try, I beg you, to get him to talk about it in his sleep by administering to him one of those mysterious homeopathic drugs and come directly to Paris to share it with us.' Cézanne was in the middle of developing his very individual system of regular parallel brushstrokes but was presumably either too taciturn or too unsure of himself to share 'recipes', so Gauguin resorted to another, simple and effective method of learning – he bought several of Cézanne's paintings. By the mid-1880s he owned no fewer than six, including a *Nature morte* and the Mediterranean landscape *Montagnes, l'Estaque*, both of which played a crucial part in his growth to maturity as a painter.

12
13

12 Paul Cézanne *Montagnes, l'Estaque c.* 1878–80

13 *Paysage provençal d'après Cézanne* 1885

14 Camille Pissarro
*Paul Gauguin sculptant
la Dame en promenade*
c. 1881

It was at the 1880 fifth Impressionist exhibition that Gauguin made his real public début as a painter. Although he included a marble bust of his wife, the group of oils he submitted seemed to rank him as a 15 landscapist, hesitantly following the example of Pissarro. Most of the critics gave him only the most dismissive of mentions. For the sixth Impressionist group exhibition the following spring, Gauguin put together a more varied range of work, including with several landscapes and still-lives a large oil study of a nude, a statuette of a Parisian woman, and a painted plaster medallion of a café-concert singer holding a bouquet. As a collector, Gauguin's tastes were not restricted, encompassing drawings of contemporary city subjects by Daumier, Forain and Degas, as well as the landscapes of Pissarro, Guillaumin and Cézanne. Gauguin's selection of exhibition works in 1881 seems to demonstrate on his part a desire not to be too readily categorized; indeed, it shows that three-dimensional work in a variety of media was an interest from the outset of his career, parallel 14 to his painting. Pissarro's drawing of Gauguin carving his statuette dates from the summer of 1881, and Gauguin claimed to have made

15 Portrait bust of Mette Gauguin, 1879

16 Bust of Clovis Gauguin, 1881

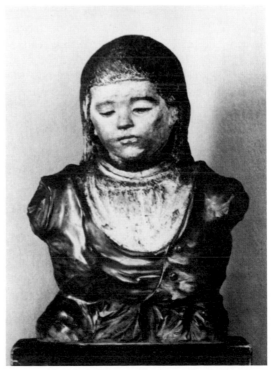

his first experiments in woodcarving at the age of seven, on the long voyage home from Peru. It had surely been no coincidence that when he and his growing family had moved to the suburb of Vaugirard in 1877, into a house at the end of a *cul de sac*, his neighbour and landlord was the sculptor Bouillot, and an adjoining studio was rented by another sculptor friend of Gauguin's, Aubé. It was here that Gauguin picked up the rudiments of clay modelling, armatures and carving, the technical knowhow that he was able to share with his master Pissarro a few years later. His earliest productions in marble, while adhering to the conventions of late nineteenth-century academic sculpture, show a remarkable plastic sense. It was not long before Gauguin was experimenting with the more adventurous media pioneered by Degas in his *Little Dancer of Fourteen Years*, first exhibited at the sixth Impressionist show in 1881. Gauguin's portrait bust of his son Clovis, which he exhibited at the seventh show in 1882, used a similarly unorthodox technical 'realism', a mixture of painted wax for the head and carved wood for the body.

16

Between 1879 and 1882 it must have been a matter of considerable anxiety for Gauguin that his work should earn the acceptance and approval of other members of the Impressionist group. Pissarro's support could, after all, be said to be coloured by a certain degree of self-interest. Among the original members of the exhibiting society, both Monet and Renoir were suspicious of his inclusion from the outset, and it was to Gauguin, among others, that Monet referred when he complained in 1880 of the formerly tight-knit little group opening its doors to all-comers and losing its essential character. In fact in 1880 and 1881, neither Monet nor Renoir exhibited with the Impressionists, submitting work to the Salon instead. Such shifting of ground, reneging on their preliminary joint declaration of independence from the Salon, was strongly opposed by Pissarro and Degas, yet it was they who had been responsible for introducing new blood into the movement – in Degas's case in the form of Federico Zandomeneghi, Mary Cassatt and Jean-François Raffaëlli.

Whatever shortcomings Gauguin may have felt as a practising artist, he was a skilful politican, his role as collector giving him a certain status, and he quickly established himself as a voice with some authority in the group. He participated vociferously in the arguments over the organization of the 1882 spring show, to the extent of 'playing the dictator' according to Eugène Manet, and campaigned

17 *La Petite rêve, étude* 1881

with Pissarro to get rid of Raffaëlli. In 1881, Raffaëlli had effectively stolen the show by his enormous submission – thirty-four paintings and drawings – which he had justified, presumably, on the grounds of their small scale. Raffaëlli specialized in representations of urban types, the rag-pickers and dispossessed of the modern city, a factor which endeared him to the naturalist writers and critics. But Gauguin argued with some justification that from a technical point of view his work had nothing to do with the concerns of Impressionism, and threatened to withdraw his own submission if Raffaëlli were to be admitted. It was a disgruntled Degas, however, who withdrew in protest at the rejection of his protégé, and as a result the 1882 show had a very different character from that of the previous year; Monet and Renoir participated once more, and landscape subjects were dominant. Gauguin's submission was almost unanimously slated in the press, although it included such unusual works as the study of his daughter Aline asleep, *La Petite rêve*, a strange foretaste of his later   17 preoccupations with the world of the unconscious.

It was perhaps Gauguin's anxiety to disassociate himself from the 'opportunistic' Raffaëlli that prevented him from enjoying the first unequivocal critical praise he received, from the pen of Joris-Karl Huysmans. A naturalist novelist and disciple of Zola, Huysmans had taken to art criticism in the late 1870s, perhaps as a way of sorting out his own aesthetic ideas. Raffaëlli, who seemed to be producing the closest visual equivalent of what Huysmans was trying to do in literature, earned his special praise, but in his review of the 1881

21 Impressionist exhibition he applauded Gauguin's *Etude de nu. Suzanne cousant* for the unswerving honesty of its execution. Gauguin had struck a vehement note of realism by representing the bodily imperfections and practical, mundane task of his model. Huysmans's admiration of Gauguin's *Etude de nu* in fact led him to launch into a diatribe against conventional treatments of the nude in contemporary art, where any attempt at realism, he argued, such as the inclusion of a discarded crinoline in Courbet's *Femme au perroquet*, was undermined by the falseness of the pose and arrangement of the subject.

Since Huysmans's various pieces of criticism seem to have remained unpublished until 1883, when he collected them in one volume entitled *L'Art Moderne*, the praise was not read by Gauguin until that year. To judge from his analysis of Huysmans's criticism in a letter to Pissarro of May 1883, he was already sure enough of himself and his ambitions by that date not to have his head turned. 'I am still flabbergasted by the fulsome flattery he throws in my face', he wrote, 'and despite its flattering side I can see that he is only seduced by the literary aspect of my nude woman and not by her qualities as a painting. We are still a long way from having a book which gives an account of Impressionist art. Would that I was a writer, I would like to produce it, there's something that needs to be done.' As well as revealing his acuity as a reader, this letter touches on concerns that would recur at various points in Gauguin's career: his mistrust of critics, his reluctance to be thought of as a literary painter and, paradoxically, his own literary and journalistic ambitions. At various stages Gauguin was to write short and more extended pieces of informal art criticism, often as an immediate response to something he had read. In fact, *L'Art Moderne* provided the catalyst for Gauguin's so-called *Notes Synthétiques* of 1884/85.

Despite the studied coolness of his reaction, Gauguin cannot fail to have been heartened by the terms of Huysmans's praise. He had been

26

described as an artist who could draw; indirectly he had been compared with Rembrandt. His wood carving had been judged modern with a touch of the gothic, which counted as high praise at a time when the virtues of the gothic were being rediscovered. Gauguin was clearly buzzing with new ideas in 1883, ideas for arranging new exhibition venues, for tackling the dealer network head on, for exploring the possibilities of Impressionist tapestry. . . . He was, therefore, not pleased to learn of the proposal, advanced primarily by Durand-Ruel, to abandon the annual Impressionist group exhibition in favour of a series of individual exhibitions at his gallery. Durand-Ruel argued that whereas the group shows sparked off much hostile publicity, one-man shows would be treated more seriously. Gauguin tried to convince Pissarro that the Impressionists' strength lay in their keeping a united front, warning him that such a development would not serve their interests, but of course it was artists such as himself and Guillaumin, artists who lacked Durand-Ruel's backing, who stood to lose most.

Gauguin's earnings on the stock market had dwindled sharply since the financial crisis of 1882, coinciding with the crash of the Union Fédérale bank. Indeed, the dampening effect of this crash had led Durand-Ruel to adopt his new, more cautious strategy of support for the Impressionists. In the face of these practical difficulties, in this first year of leaner living, Gauguin finally decided to 'take the bull by the horns', as he put it, and commit himself wholeheartedly to an artistic career. Painting had been increasingly occupying his thoughts and his time, and he felt he no longer had the energy to keep two careers going in tandem. Gauguin calculated that he would soon compensate for the immediate loss of income by putting all his business sense into conquering the art market. He was confident that with the right administrative skills and the right contacts, both of which he had, painting could be a viable enterprise. Pissarro was at first bowled over by this determination and courage on Gauguin's part. It was not long, however, before he grew more sceptical of Gauguin's commercialism in general and in particular of his professed special understanding of the bourgeois public.

Gauguin's greatest difficulty, he well knew, was going to be supporting and holding together his family. His wife, he ruefully acknowledged, could not cope with financial hardship. Two years before, they had been living in considerable style, with servants, a

18   comfortable house and garden in the rue Carcel, as recorded in several
of his Vaugirard paintings. Now they would need to find cheaper
accommodation out of Paris. In October 1883 when he broached the
subject of a move to Rouen with Mette, the family consisted of four
children with a fifth on the way. From every point of view Gauguin
had timed his change of career badly.

After less than a year of a cramped and uncomfortable existence in
Rouen, where the bourgeois buyers turned out to be more elusive
than Gauguin had predicted, Mette removed herself and two of the
children to Copenhagen. Emil, the eldest, had already been sent there
to receive the benefit of a Danish education. Gauguin shamefacedly
followed a month or so later with the two others.

The motives that led this apparently successful businessman to
sacrifice family and career to the elusive dream of becoming a painter
were given literary elaboration as early as 1919 in Somerset
Maugham's best-selling novel *The Moon and Sixpence*. Some thirty
years later, an edition of the artist's letters to his wife, which began
with their first separation in 1885 and continued until 1894, revealed a
more enduring marital relationship and more complex set of
motivations than Maugham had imagined for his fictional hero
Strickland. Nevertheless, one suspects that, as for Mrs Strickland, it
was several years before Mette Gauguin realized that painting was a
threat to her happiness which she was powerless to fight. She was not
unappreciative of her husband's breadth of artistic talent – later she
was astounded by the quality of the works he sent home from Tahiti –
but at this early stage she could not understand or forgive his
seemingly demonic urge not just to paint, but to produce intractable,
unsaleable works. She might have adjusted well enough had Gauguin
been turning out safe, accessible *plein air* landscapes like her
Norwegian brother-in-law Fritz Thaulow, for whom, incidentally,
Gauguin had nothing but scorn. But she was aware of the demands
the life of artistic independence made on families like the Pissarros, of
whom she had become fond, and was not prepared to martyr her own
or her children's lives and well-being to the uncertainties of such an
existence, to throw up the security, respectability, sociability and
education which she held dear.

The differences of experience and upbringing that existed at the
very outset of the Gauguins' marriage made it difficult to ride out this
storm, particularly as Gauguin seems to have fallen for the

28

18 *Intérieur du peintre à Paris, rue Carcel* 1881

nineteenth-century notion that artistic genius could not thrive in the shackles of normal social ties and responsibilities. Given the circumstances, he and Mette remained remarkably close, determined up to the last to make a go of the separate lives they embarked on in 1885, to get Gauguin launched as a painter with a steady income in order that they and their children should benefit and resume family life. Being one-sided, Gauguin's letters to his wife touch on some, but probably not all of the issues involved. They bear witness to alternating rancour and tenderness, anger and resentment at emotional and sexual rejection, self-justifications dissolving into dashed hopes, self-pitying recriminations and frustrated paternal feelings. Confident calculations, predictions and taunts led to misunderstandings and ensuing bitterness over money, and it was these that finally led Mette to break off communications in 1894.

19 *Nature morte au profil de Laval* 1886

CHAPTER TWO

The Full-Time Painter (1885–1888)

While living with his in-laws in the picturesque but unwelcoming city of Copenhagen, various inconveniences prevented Gauguin from getting on with his painting. The long cold winter effectively ruled out *plein air* landscape work, the available oil colours were inferior to those in Paris, and the Gad family, for whom Gauguin was a virtual stranger, disapproved of his painting at all. Although he had made his resolve to devote himself solely to art, the impossibility of earning money in this way had forced him to compromise and for a period in early 1885 he ostensibly worked as agent for a French tarpaulin manufacturer. It is doubtful whether many of the deals he tried to set up came to anything. For one thing, he spoke no Scandinavian languages and had to rely on his brother-in-law to sound out the Norwegian market. In any case, he was much more occupied by the problems of picture-making, as he tackled scenes in and around Copenhagen or still-lives indoors. The occasional news about the art world in Paris which he received from newspapers and from faithful friends was a lifeline.

To Gauguin's surprise, he found that his connections with the Paris Impressionists carried some weight in the provincial Danish context and as a result his work generated a degree of interest and gossip, whether in the form of disapproval from the more conservative figures of the art establishment or secret emulation from the younger men. No doubt he exaggerated the shocking impact his reputation for 'impiety' made on this puritanical, hidebound society, a society whose gentility is merely glimpsed through the doorway in his *Nature morte dans un intérieur*. Certainly, he exaggerated or simply 20 misunderstood the situation when an exhibition of his paintings, held in May 1885 under the auspices of the Society of the Friends of Art, lasted only five days; his exhibition was not closed with peremptory haste, as he believed, for this was the normal length of the Society's exhibitions; it was, however, passed over in the Copenhagen press, which suggests a certain cold-shouldering of the outsider to which

20 *Nature morte dans un intérieur* 1885

Gauguin was quick to take exception. His attitude to the Danes remained sour for the rest of his life. In fact, his experiences in Copenhagen led Gauguin to describe himself for the first, but by no means for the last, time as one of the 'martyrs' of painting. The self-portrait, *Gauguin devant son chevalet*, externalized this mood, playing up the image of the bohemian artist, isolated in his garret.

The frustration of life in Denmark and of being absent from the heart of things in Paris, as indeed he was to be for most of the remainder of his career, seems to have had a positive side; it helped to clarify Gauguin's thinking about art and to crystallize his ambitions. This was a period when he studied his own collection of pictures closely. Writing to an artist friend, Emile Schuffenecker, he observed that just as one could read character from hand-writing, so an artist's temperament could be deciphered from his marks and style. An artist such as Cézanne, he argued, judging from his fondness for heavy, passive forms and deep intense colours, and from his widely-spaced handwriting, had a mystic, contemplative, oriental nature. In a letter

21 *Etude de nu. Suzanne cousant* 1880

dated May 1885, he imparted some of his technical ideas to Pissarro, who had recently criticized the dull tonalities from which he felt Gauguin's Rouen landscapes suffered. Gauguin sounded remarkably sure of where he was heading, arguing that these dull effects were a necessary stage in his determination to achieve an unvariegated overall surface, a matt quality which was the very *opposite* of the slick, eye-catching surfaces he so disliked in the work of many contemporaries. He presumably meant such artists as Gervex and Bastien-Lepage whose influence was marked in the work of the Danish artists. Whether or not he was yet fully conscious of the consequence, the ambition to paint in this broad, matt way would involve following a very different course from the one Pissarro was currently advocating – the use of small, even, but separate touches to achieve an overall unity. It was some years before the anti-Impressionistic effects Gauguin had in mind were visibly realized in his paintings. For the time being, perhaps to mollify Pissarro, whose advice he seemed to be rejecting, he spoke with satisfaction of having attained a lighter, more flexible execution in his latest efforts to capture the first greens of spring. The comparison between his own work and the timid efforts of the Danes had confirmed him in the belief that mediocrity was the greatest scourge of art; there was no need to be afraid of producing an 'exaggerated' art; on the contrary, extremism offered the only real way forward.

Gauguin used exactly this argument about the positive quality of exaggeration in art in his *Notes Synthétiques*, a factor which makes a date of 1884/85 for these writings a certainty. Indeed, there were contemporary reasons for his focusing on the question; 'exaggeration' was a charge that had frequently been levelled in the past at Delacroix and at the romantics in general. Delacroix's posthumous reputation was just then in the process of being salvaged, somewhat tardily, in a major retrospective exhibition at the Ecole des Beaux-Arts. A great admirer of Delacroix, Gauguin was furious at having to miss this event, and was avid for reports of it, even asking a friend to purchase on his behalf a photograph of Delacroix's *Shipwreck of Don Juan*. Now that the genius of Delacroix had been officially sanctioned, most of the reviewers were put in the awkward position of trying to justify the hostility of former critics to Delacroix's supposed excesses.

It is surely no coincidence that the arguments Gauguin advanced in his *Notes* echoed the well-known precepts of Delacroix: the

22 *Le Port de Rouen* 1884

important role of colour in drawing, the science of colour harmony and the relation between painting and music. Gauguin contended that the expressive means at the disposal of the writer and musician were inferior to the range of colour and tonal variation available to the painter, a range so mind-boggling in complexity (albeit simpler than nature herself) that any critic presuming to judge a painting would need to have some prior instruction in the science of colour as well as 'special sensations of nature'. This jibe was directly aimed at Huysmans who had 'ignorantly' complained of the over-use of blue in the paintings of the Impressionists. The merits of juxtaposing pure colours, as opposed to using impure mixed colours, and the interdependence and inseparability of colour and line were Gauguin's chief themes. One could describe them as anti-academic pre-occupations that followed on naturally enough from his involvement with Impressionism, but they were also highly topical ones; indeed, they were exercising the theoretical mind of another new member of the Paris avant-garde, Georges Seurat, at this very time.

23 *Les Maraîchers de Vaugirard c.* 1879

Gauguin knew he as yet lacked the necessary mechanical expertise and manual dexterity to put his ideas into practice, but he was sure he could remedy this by sheer hard work and repeated exercises. 'Don't perspire over a picture, a strong emotion can be translated immediately: dream on it and seek its simplest form.' This typically romantic self-admonition was passed on as advice to Schuffenecker. Emile Schuffenecker, like Gauguin, was a disaffected stockbroker who had taken the decision to become a full-time painter. (It is worth noting in passing how many of Gauguin's future associates in the art world had previously followed other callings; his case was by no means unique. There were Guillaumin, Vincent Van Gogh and Meyer de Haan among the painters, Octave Mirbeau, another former stockbroker, among the critics.) The great advantage Schuffenecker had over Gauguin was a steady investment income. He had put a large inheritance into a profitable gold business, which enabled him to survive in comfort as an independent painter, despite his modest talent, a fact that increasingly rankled Gauguin. He had sunk his own

36

24 *Végétation tropicale, Martinique* 1887

capital into a much more risky commodity, modern painting; although occasional sales of pictures helped him to survive at critical moments, his collection needed more time to mature before it could count as a successful investment. Gauguin had even made some mysterious speculation in Spanish painting, whereby he hoped to make money out of a victory for the revolutionary party in the current political struggles there. He served as a clandestine courier on one or two occasions between 1885 and 1886, but power remained in the hands of Spain's ruling party and the hoped-for financial gains were not forthcoming. Given their common backgrounds and joint commitment to independent painting, it was naturally to 'good old Schuff' that Gauguin turned in a crisis. The family situation in Denmark became so awkward and rancorous by the summer of 1885 that he decided to return to Paris, intending to work on whatever jobs he could find, at least until he should manage, as he put it, to carve himself a niche in the art market. His wife and children remained in Copenhagen, apart from Clovis who accompanied him. They had Mette's family and friends for support and Mette could earn some income from translation work and French teaching.

After spending a few weeks in Dieppe and making a flying visit to London, Gauguin spent a cold and uncomfortable winter in rented accommodation in Paris, selling part of his collection to Durand-Ruel and earning a few francs by sticking posters in the railway stations. Clovis fell ill, and eventually Gauguin's sister stepped in, providing the necessary funds to instal him in a boarding school.

From 1883 to 1886 Gauguin scarcely devoted more time to his art than he had done previously when in full-time employment. The disruptive moves and the restless search for the next meal left him little time or concentration for his painting. It was thus hardly surprising that the group of works he submitted to the long-delayed eighth Impressionist exhibition, held in the spring of 1886 in the rue Laffitte, marked very little stylistic development from 1882, rather a narrowing down of his artistic range. He sent in eighteen canvases, fourteen of them landscapes, and only one wooden sculpture. There was a consensus of critical opinion about Gauguin that year. His work showed conscientious effort, even a latent talent, but his landscapes were somewhat monotonous, their heavy, brooding atmospheres suggesting to the critic Paul Adam the malevolent powers of nature. With hindsight, we can say that these were appropriate words to have

38

25 *Vaches au repos* 1885

chosen. Beside the several views of farmyards and meadows, including *Vaches au repos*, his small canvas of *Baigneuses à Dieppe* must 25, 29 have stood out as something rather different: again, with hindsight we can see it as the first instance of a recurring theme, the woman in the waves. Stylistically, too, it oddly presaged later works with its single, strong horizontal band of emerald green for the distant sea and the dance-like arrangement of the four female silhouettes in the foreground.

The relationship between avant-garde art and literature was cemented in 1886. One of the lengthier reviews of the Impressionist exhibition was penned by Félix Fénéon, a young critic with an eye to future trends. He was of the new generation of poets and writers who were growing tired of the naturalist creed and its endless fascination with the seamy side of contemporary life. Under the banner of Symbolism, they wanted to create a new poetry of evocation and idea, nuance and suggestion, and they were looking for signs that artists would move in a parallel direction. In his review, Fénéon gave due credit to Gauguin for the unusual density of his colour, but

26 Breton Girl (Study for *Les Quatre Bretonnes*), 1886

27 Vase with Breton Girls, 1886–7

classified him with Guillaumin, Monet and Sisley as one of the adherents to the original, arbitrary procedures of Impressionism. Ultimately, his praise and attention were given to Seurat and his group, whom he was shortly to dub the Neo-Impressionists, and their radical overhaul of Impressionist technique. He wrote at length about Seurat's huge canvas *Un Dimanche d'Été à l'Île de la Grande Jatte*, 28 explaining the theoretical rationale for treating luminous atmospheres by means of dots of pure colour, and hailed Seurat for going beyond the 'fleeting glimpses' of Impressionism and setting down a more permanent synthesis of nature. There was no doubt that Fénéon saw Seurat as the key figure for the future of avant-garde painting.

Gauguin must have had Fénéon's article among others in mind when he wrote to his wife in June 1886, in surprisingly optimistic tones, that their exhibition had 'once again brought the whole question of Impressionism up for discussion, and favourably'. The lukewarm critical reactions to his own works seem to have acted on him like a spur, partly, no doubt, because he was basically unsympathetic to the ideas and pictures that had won most of the honours. Georges Seurat, placed now in a position of authority, was not a generous young man. A situation arose in the studios of Montmartre that summer that highlighted a growing state of tension between Seurat and Gauguin, and left bitter feelings on both sides. Having been offered the use of Signac's studio while Signac was away, Gauguin found his entry was challenged by Seurat, who occupied the adjacent studio. Angry letters were exchanged, Gauguin was accused of being boorish, Guillaumin and Pissarro were appealed to. Finally, in a fit of pique, Gauguin complained to Signac, 'I may be a hesitant and unlearned artist, but as a man of the world *I will allow no one* to mess me about.'

Time was short for Gauguin if, at the age of thirty-eight, he was to achieve his grand ambitions, and he clearly felt threatened by the new rage for the 'little dot' that took hold in 1886. To his dismay, it had already swept up Pissarro, and Schuffenecker was just one of many independent painters who, lacking Gauguin's resolve and confidence and anxious to be in the swim, converted from a loosely Impressionist technique to a variant of pointillism in the wake of the 1886 exhibition. Although Gauguin turned out one or two dotted canvases himself, no doubt to satisfy his curiosity, he made no secret of his disdain for 'scientific' Impressionism.

28 Georges Seurat *Un Dimanche d'Eté à l'Ile de la Grande Jatte* 1884–6

Gauguin turned down the chance to exhibit again with the Neo-Impressionists that year, either at the Independents' salon or at a group show in Nantes. Instead, he decided to make Brittany his location for the summer. This move represented a disassociation from the art circles he had hitherto frequented and relied on: Pissarro already considered his one-time pupil to have defected to the rival camp of the so-called 'romantic' Impressionists, because of his rejection of the pointillist option, and he predicted that agreement between them would henceforth be difficult.

Brittany was the favourite summer destination for art students from the teaching studios in Paris and months before Gauguin had spoken of his intention of taking up summer residence there, attracted like everyone else by its reputation for cheapness. What expectations Gauguin had of the pretty village of Pont-Aven as a place to paint would be hard to say. Certainly, he did not have quite the same objectives as most of the cosmopolitan group of artists who flocked there annually. He had hitherto shown no interest in painting

42

29 *Baigneuses à Dieppe* 1885

folkloric, antiquated customs, for instance, and working peasant figures had featured only marginally in his landscapes. As for the well-known strength of religious faith among the Breton people, it is doubtful whether Gauguin would yet have seen picturesque religious ceremonies as potential subjects, though they had clearly proved to be popular for the contemporary Salon painter Pascal Dagnan- 32 Bouveret.

Apart from having the freedom and time to paint landscapes under the still 'revolutionary' banner of Impressionism, Gauguin's only fixed artistic objective was to work on ceramics that winter in Paris with Ernest Chaplet, an employee of the expanding Haviland studio. Gauguin had been introduced to Chaplet by the Impressionist exhibitor Félix Bracquemond, himself a keen ceramicist. Even before leaving Paris, Gauguin had begun work on recycling and simplifying motifs used in earlier works. In Brittany, his concentration on drawing, particularly on spare, simplified drawings of figure and animal motifs, related to his plans for ceramic decoration. It is

probable that Gauguin had already seen how Kate Greenaway's children's illustrations had been adapted for decorative use on
30 ceramics at the Haviland studio, and he also knew the children's drawings of Randolph Caldecott, whose artistic pilgrimage through Brittany had preceded Gauguin's arrival by some eight years. The deliberately naïve style of these successful British illustrators (admired by Pissarro and praised by Huysmans in *L'Art Moderne*) seemed appropriate to the rural motifs and quaint costumes that presented themselves to Gauguin in Pont-Aven.

His more resolved colour drawings were a basis from which he
26 later worked up painted compositions in the studio, using for the first time large-scale figures in a landscape setting. His most important
31 1886 Breton picture, *Les Quatre Bretonnes*, was painted from drawings
35 back in Paris during the winter, as was the large *Deux baigneuses* of 1887. So established was Pont-Aven as an artists' colony that the village women expected to earn extra money through modelling, and Gauguin's sense of artistic 'otherness' did not extend to rejecting what was on offer. The importance of drawing as a way of achieving

30 Vase in the manner of Kate Greenaway, made in the studio of Ernest Chaplet for the Haviland firm, *c.* 1884

32 (OPPOSITE) Pascal Dagnan-Bouveret *Breton Women at a Pardon* 1887

31 *Les Quatre Bretonnes* 1886

33 Edgar Degas *Femme nue debout* c. 1880–3   34 Study for *Deux baigneuses* 1886–7

simplicity and strength in a composition was a lesson Gauguin had
already learned from Pissarro, and it was reinforced by Degas's
33 impressive group of nudes drawn in pastel which had been exhibited
at the 1886 eighth Impressionist show. It was these artists' examples
that were foremost in Gauguin's mind when he worked on his large
34 pastel drawings from posed Breton figures. Not content to record
unfamiliar dress and Celtic physiognomy, Gauguin tackled the sort of
awkward, arresting poses favoured by Degas, a woman seen from
behind, arms akimbo, for example, another foreshortened and in
profile, adjusting her shoe. Gauguin spent time studying the nude as
37 well, but his oil painting *Jeunes Bretons au bain*, which was painted
directly *en plein air* and used one of the most complex figural
arrangements Gauguin had so far essayed, displayed a curious mish-
mash of influences. Cézannesque in subject, it was strongly indebted

46

35 *Deux baigneuses* 1887

36 *La Bergère Bretonne* 1886

to Degas in design and boldly painted in spots of pure colour. Also somewhat confused in composition and technique was *La Bergère Bretonne*, a painting for which Gauguin made numerous small, individual drawings in his sketchbook. It is possible that this was one of the paintings he prepared quite carefully in the studio, before taking the canvas out of doors. But the striations of bright colour, probably added as a final touch with a fine sable brush, seem to militate against the generally uniform, dense tones employed in the landscape.

Works such as these evidently scandalized the other itinerant artists, and just as he had in Copenhagen, Gauguin revelled in his capacity to provoke outrage. He admitted to being gingered up by the proximity of easily offended conservatives. According to two separate witness accounts, the reason Gauguin attracted attention during his three-month stay was as much due to his outlandish looks, demeanour and pugilistic prowess as to his strange manner of painting. Considerably older, more experienced and more widely

37 *Jeunes Bretons au bain* 1886

travelled than most of the student-age residents, Gauguin had a certain authority and when he pronounced on artistic matters he was attended. The disciple who attached himself most closely to Gauguin was Charles Laval, a former pupil of Bonnat, and his studious profile appears at the right edge of Gauguin's *Nature morte au profil de Laval.* 19 In colouring, the painting pays homage to Cézanne, but it also characteristically contrives to include an unexpected item, in this case one of Gauguin's ceramic pots. It is likely that the painting was completed in Paris.

Gauguin's finances were still in a critical state when he returned from Brittany, and a month in hospital, caused by an acute attack of angina, left him completely out of pocket, despondent and bitter at the start of 1887. However, the studies he had brought back furnished him with ideas for his ceramics and in the space of a month, working alongside Chaplet in the rue Blomet in Vaugirard, he turned out fifty-five pieces of pottery. The energy he expended in this output was formidable and only explicable in view of his high hopes of

making money from the sale of ceramics. The series included some
27   functional, conventionally-shaped pieces, the cylindrical *Vase with
Breton Girls*, for example, in which for the first time Gauguin
employed the cloisonnist technique of flat areas of colour, demarcated
by firm lines, here incised and gilded. Another important piece was a
40   *Jardinière*, elaborately painted and glazed with modelled figures and
animals, the same ones he had used in *La Bergère Bretonne*. But most of
the pots were stranger and cruder, like the stoneware jug or the pot
represented in the *Nature morte*, hand-modelled and reminiscent in
form of the pre-Columbian pottery he had known from his
38, 39   childhood in Peru. In these, Gauguin stretched the medium to its
limits, exploiting its primitive connotations, and the unconventional
results were, with some reservations, admired by Chaplet,
Bracquemond and others. However, not surprisingly, they proved
difficult to sell, and once again Gauguin's optimistic forecast turned
out to be ill-founded.

By the spring of 1887 Gauguin's financial situation was desperate
and his only thought was to escape from the miasma of debt and
recrimination in which he found himself. A short-lived panic in Paris
about a possible war with Germany was seized on by Gauguin as a
potential way out of the impasse, but it was a false alarm. Entrusting
the pots to his colour merchant Arsène Portier, with Charles Laval
Gauguin joined a ship bound for America in April, planning to hole
up on the island of Taboga in the Pacific and there renew his physical
strength. Plans went awry, and Gauguin felt he had no alternative but
to earn his passage back to the Caribbean island of Martinique by
working as a navvy on the Panama canal, then under construction.
Laval and Gauguin had glimpsed Martinique, which was a French
protectorate, on their journey out and it had struck them as offering a
41   paradise for the painter. The climate, the landscape, the brilliantly
coloured flora and fauna and the easy-going native population
proved to be as enchanting as they had imagined. They rented a negro
hut and set to work with a will. Unfortunately, Gauguin had
contracted dysentery while working in Panama so that, despite the
new attack and enthusiasm he felt ready to bring to his painting, and
his attraction to the possibilities of colonial life, his energies were
progressively sapped by the illness. At the end of a four-month stay,
after sending a series of pitiful letters to his wife and Schuffenecker, he
returned to Paris, in worse physical shape than when he had left.

38 Cup decorated with the figure of a bathing girl, 1888

39 Vase decorated with the half-length figure of a woman, exhibited 1893

40 Rectangular Jardinière, 1887

Gauguin judged the dozen or so canvases he brought back with him to be far better than his Pont-Aven work. Certainly, they are characterized by a greater degree of freedom and boldness in drawing and colour juxtapositions; Gauguin's already established fondness for dense, airless effects, and strong reds set against greens, was appropriate to the tropical vegetation and began to work effectively in a painting such as *Les Mangos, Martinique*, one of the four works in which he included substantial figures. The poses of the two negresses in the foreground carry a strength and conviction that is powerfully expressed in the preparatory drawing, and there is nothing casual about their insertion into the composition, whose spatial intervals and balancing vertical and horizontal accents have been carefully considered. It works both as a linear and as a colouristic design, the small striations giving the painting something of the quality of a tapestry, the medium in which Gauguin had been so keen to experiment a few years earlier. He achieved a similar surface richness in *Allées et venues, Martinique*, a painting later owned by Degas, and in the pure landscape *Végétation tropicale, Martinique*.

These pictures were seen and enthused over at Portier's gallery in Paris by two Dutchmen, Theo and Vincent Van Gogh. Gauguin's encounter with the Van Gogh brothers in late 1887 was to have important implications, as he was not slow to realize. Theo Van Gogh was a picture dealer who had been employed by the Goupil firm (later known as Boussod, Valadon and Co.) in Paris for nine years. Sharing an apartment block in Montmartre with Portier, the colour merchant who had been acting in a spasmodic way as dealer on Gauguin's behalf, Theo had met other clients of Portier's, the Pisarros father and son, and Guillaumin. Recently, he himself had begun to take an interest in selling the work of these independent painters. Indeed, since 1886 he had succeeded in infiltrating a few works by Degas, Pissarro and others into the upstairs showroom of Goupil's gallery in the boulevard Montmartre, and was striving hard to introduce them to the firm's clientèle, who were more used to the work of accredited Salon artists. He was spurred on by the encouragement of his elder brother Vincent, who had arrived in Paris in 1886 from The Hague, anxious to further his artistic career. Vincent Van Gogh quickly established contacts with a wider group of artists, fellow pupils from the Cormon studio such as Emile Bernard, Henri de Toulouse-Lautrec and Louis Anquetin, and others such as

41 *Bord de mer, Martinique* 1887

42 *Allées et venues, Martinique* 1887

43 Two Women from Martinique, 1887

44 *Les Mangos, Martinique* 1887

Paul Signac and Lucien Pissaro. Undoubtedly, Vincent helped to extend his brother's knowledge of the most recent trends in painting. Theo had made overtures to Camille Pissarro in the autumn of 1887, aware that the painter's new pointillist technique was not finding favour with Durand-Ruel, and in December 1887, on the strength of seeing the Martinique works, he offered to take on a small group of Gauguin's recent canvases, to hang next to those of Pissarro and Guillaumin. Gauguin was of course delighted, particularly as he had as yet failed to elicit any sort of firm business commitment from another dealer. He made much of the importance of the new arrangement in a letter to Mette of December 1887, stressing that the gallery's central address, unlike Portier's, would mean that exhibits had a better chance of catching the attention of the public and the critics. Indeed, through the gallery he had already sold paintings to the value of 900 francs. It was becoming, so he boasted, the 'centre for the Impressionists'.

Gauguin was an optimist and had the capacity to respond immediately to the slimmest of favourable augurs. His endeavours were receiving endorsement from an important practical quarter. This was just the fillip he needed at a time when his health and strength were weakened. There is no question that he now had a will to work, but he was equally convinced that for him, as for Vincent Van Gogh, Paris was not the best place to work in. It was too expensive, it involved too much wrangling and money grubbing, there were too many diversions and the stimulus of new ideas, constantly fermenting among the younger artists, could be counter-productive. Writing to Mette early in 1888, he explained that as he was on the point of being launched, he needed, over the next seven or eight months, to make a 'supreme effort' for his painting. Just as Van Gogh left Paris for Provence, Gauguin left Paris in early February for Brittany, and took up residence once again, at the Pension Gloanec, in Pont-Aven.

45 *Hiver, ou petit Breton arrangeant son sabot* 1888

CHAPTER THREE

Collaborative Experiments (1888)

A few weeks after arriving in Brittany, once the weather and his health permitted, Gauguin set about his campaign. He now had a much clearer notion of what Brittany could offer him as a painter. He wanted to 'imbue himself with the character of the people and of the landscape'. He contrasted his own interests with the 'Parisianist' preoccupations of his old comrade Schuffenecker. Whereas Schuffenecker was now caught up in the sort of modern social theme favoured by the Neo-Impressionist group (and currently tackling the subject of road-menders), Gauguin felt more at home with the rustic: 'When my clogs resound on this granite soil, I hear the dull, matt, powerful tone that I'm after in painting. . . .' Were it not for that renewed insistence on the 'dull, matt, powerful tone' (a foreglimpse of the crude primitive qualities he was soon consciously and assertively to set against the sophisticated, slick, photographic finish of contemporary Salon painters), there would be nothing to differentiate Gauguin's ambitions from those of the numerous other peasant and rural painters working throughout the regions of France in the 1880s. It was a widely held belief that the Bretons had somehow retained their primitive, Celtic character and that this was due to their harsh existence at the mercy of the elements, toiling at the unyielding granite rock of their peninsula. Arriving in Pont-Aven in winter doubtless made Gauguin more aware of the underlying harshness of the terrain than he had been two years before.

The painting season had not yet opened so Gauguin was temporarily free of distracting influences and could pick up the threads of his development as a painter from where he had left off in Martinique. In *Hiver, ou petit Breton arrangeant son sabot*, one of the earlier works done in 1888, Gauguin continued to use the combination of loosely Impressionistic technique, heightened colour and Degas-like figure drawing. The vertical composition faithfully conveys the cramped, intimate feel of the steeply wooded valley of the Aven, with the church and town glimpsed through the still-bare

45

46 *La Ronde des petites Bretonnes* 1888

trees, but the action of the boy in clogs, surely included as a sign of 'Bretonness', carries echoes of the ballet context from which the pose was taken. An uncharacteristically luminous and delicate spring
48   landscape, *Les Premières fleurs, les Bretonnes aux Avins*, exemplifies Gauguin's continuing stylistic equivocation; although unscientific and unvariegated, the small vertical dabs of brushwork seem to have been inspired to some degree by pointillism. He was not yet approaching the powerful, matt simplicity of which he had spoken. Ironically, this particular canvas was well received in Paris, and later in the year there was talk of Degas buying it. A work in which Gauguin felt he had achieved a more essentially Breton character was
46   *La Ronde des petites Bretonnes*, painted in June 1888 and inspired by the traditional celebrations at hay-making time. Some of the dance forms evidently harked back to druidic festivals, and one senses that here

58

47 *Lutte Bretonne* 1888

48 *Les Premières fleurs, les Bretonnes aux Avins* 1888

Gauguin was starting to attune himself to those archaic aspects of Breton life that had long epitomized the romance of Brittany for poets and painters. *La Ronde*, thanks no doubt to its quaint though rather sentimental and hackneyed theme, proved readily marketable, attracting attention from various quarters and selling eventually for 500 francs to a client of Theo Van Gogh's.

It was not until July, however, when Pont-Aven had once again been invaded by the 'band of simpletons' from Paris who considered Gauguin a madman, that he could congratulate himself on having struck a truly original and independent note in his painting, on having gone beyond anything he had achieved before. After working on a series of studies of boys bathing, his nudes, so he claimed, were now 47 'not at all Degas-like'. The latest, *Lutte Bretonne* or *Enfants luttant*, showed a fight between two lads by the river, no doubt limbering up

60

for the traditional wrestling bouts that took place after the religious pardons. Essentially Breton though the subject was, its treatment was 'absolutely Japanese by a savage from Peru', he explained to Schuffenecker. In a letter posted at much the same time to Vincent Van Gogh, he included a sketch of the composition.

As these letters make clear, there was no question of Gauguin's working in a vacuum just because he was installed among strangers in Pont-Aven, nor of his forgetting his artistic pedigree. Japonism was then a live issue among the younger artists in Paris; Vincent Van Gogh had organized an exhibition of his own substantial collection of Japanese prints in Montmartre that winter, and his correspondence was full of references to the Japanese printmakers. Gauguin's mention of Degas indicates that he was still conscious of the elder Impressionist as a powerful but sometimes oppressive presence looking over his shoulder. In fact, shortly before leaving Paris, Gauguin would have seen his own painting *Deux baigneuses* hanging in the Goupil gallery 35 next to the latest Degas pastels of women in their bathtubs, an interesting contrast between contemporary rural and urban interpretations of the nude theme. Gauguin made a series of small 50 copies of the Degas pastels in his sketchbook, and re-used a number of the daring, often ungainly poses in later works. Gauguin's letters from Brittany also reveal, indirectly, how close a watch he kept over his critical status in Paris. Certainly, he took considerable note of the writings of Félix Fénéon, now established as regular art correspondent, with a monthly calendar, for *La Revue Indépendante*. Fénéon wrote at length about *Deux baigneuses* and several of the Degas nudes in the February edition. Earlier, he had praised Gauguin's rare skill as a potter, but there had been a sting in the tail: Fénéon had described Gauguin as *grièche*, an arcane word loosely translatable as sore-headed or unpleasant. This set down publicly and for posterity the reputation for awkwardness Gauguin had earned himself in his dealings with fellow artists in Paris. The slight to his character, far from passing unnoticed or unfelt, was referred to on several occasions by him in letters that year. It is significant that from this date onwards Gauguin cultivated the image of himself as a 'savage from Peru', which was in a sense a way of acknowledging and excusing his ungentlemanly reputation.

Despite Fénéon's reservations about Gauguin's personality, he was the first critic consistently to draw attention to Gauguin's art, and in

49 Edgar Degas *Danseuse ajustant son soulier c.* 1880

May 1888 he was arguing that a Gauguin one-man show was now due, believing it would reveal what a 'powerful and isolated artist' he was. Such support must have considerably boosted Gauguin's confidence. Nor was it an idle suggestion. *La Revue Indépendante* had a small space in its offices where a number of exhibitions were arranged throughout 1888, the artists involved ranging from Manet, who had died in 1883, and the fashionable Besnard, to men such as Guillaumin, Pissarro, Seurat, Signac, Luce and Dubois-Pillet, the last five all adherents of Neo-Impressionism. Sure enough, in November 1888, an application from Schuffenecker having been rejected, an invitation to mount his first ever Paris one-man show was sent instead to Gauguin, no doubt at Fénéon's behest. But it is a measure of Gauguin's proud, combative and unforgiving nature that he turned this invitation down, partly out of loyalty to Schuffenecker, but more importantly on the grounds that the *La Revue Indépendante* editorial board was fundamentally antagonistic towards him, and he was not going to be seen compromising with the enemy camp. His letter of refusal, although ostensibly humble and self-deprecating, was heavily

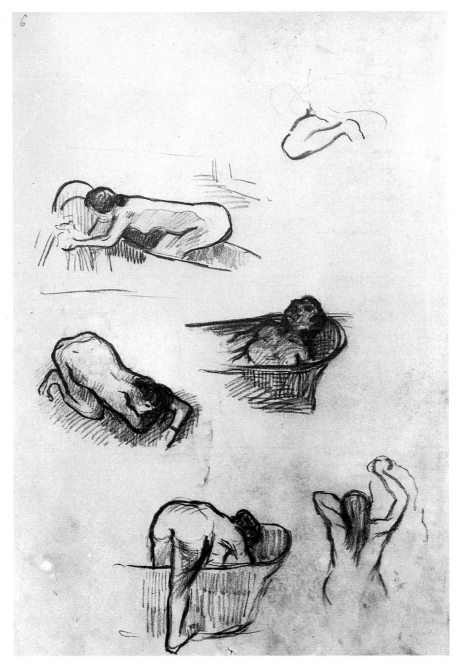

50 Page of sketches after Degas, *c.* 1888–9

loaded with irony. 'Feeling for the past three years that my strengths as an artist were nowhere near sufficient to keep up with the modern progress being introduced among the Impressionists who've so rapidly been replaced by the Neo-Impressionists, I have resolved to work on my own, away from all group publicity. – My studies of the tropics are insufficient as exact records of nature and I believe *La Revue Indépendante* will be powerless to give them the clarity and luminosity they lack. . . .' For all his professed indifference to critical opinion and disdain for the views of literary men, this letter reveals, on the contrary, how susceptible Gauguin was to criticism; rather than suffering in silence as the equally touchy Cézanne would have done, he could not resist rising to the bait.

By the time he received this invitation, Gauguin had in fact already accepted another, to exhibit in February 1889 with the enterprising Belgian independent artistic organization, Les Vingt. Gauguin planned to stage an open assault on the 'little dot' there, knowing that his works would be seen and compared with the latest works of Seurat. Despite his claims to be shunning all group publicity, it is clear that Gauguin kept himself informed of the latest initiatives within the Parisian avant-garde. Although the letters to Theo and Vincent Van Gogh, which began early in 1888, were initially concerned with strictly practical and commercial matters, over the months they revealed Gauguin's increasing need for a sympathetic ear, and his deliberate construction of an artistic persona. He was seeking to impress himself on their mercies as a brilliant, but maligned and suffering genius for whom encouragement, sales and support were a life-line. In order to provide that support, as well as companionship for his brother Vincent, Theo hit on the scheme of persuading Gauguin to leave Pont-Aven and instead share studio space and living expenses with Vincent in Arles. This involved delicate negotiation; Vincent was enthusiastic but nervous about the plan; Gauguin presented himself as by no means unwilling, yet prevaricated throughout the summer months, pleading poverty and debts in Pont-Aven and proposing alternative measures for keeping artists such as themselves in pocket, a sort of artist/dealer co-operative with himself as administrator and Theo as dealer. He allowed himself to play the prima donna, confident that this promised financial act of faith on the part of Theo Van Gogh was a sound indication of the dealer's high estimation of his work, even though sales continued to elude him.

Prompted by Vincent's tendency to give a detailed literary commentary of his work in progress, Gauguin had begun to reciprocate. He expounded not only his general artistic principles (for instance, his endorsement of Vincent's view that exactitude had no importance in art, that art was essentially an 'abstraction' from nature which had to be pondered and then simplified) but also, for the first time in his career, analysed what he considered the more important paintings he was working on. This very activity of describing in words the technique, style and underlying meaning of his works arguably encouraged Gauguin in the direction of a more self-conscious, literary art: in short, pushed him towards Symbolism. His correspondence with Vincent Van Gogh in the summer of 1888 was crucial to Gauguin's consciousness and subsequent construction of himself as a Synthetist and Symbolist.

There was another, possibly more important, catalyst that encouraged Gauguin's recognition of his true artistic direction that summer. Emile Bernard, a precociously talented and intense young man, formerly a student with Van Gogh and Anquetin at the

52 Emile Bernard *Les Bretonnes dans la prairie* 1888

Cormon studio, came to Pont-Aven on Vincent's advice to seek out
Gauguin. They had met each other there two years before, without
any useful exchanges or meeting of minds. On this occasion, Bernard
knew more what to expect of Gauguin and approached him in the
spirit of an admirer. Gauguin for his part was immediately impressed
by the work Bernard had brought with him from Saint-Briac, some
highly simplified primitive drawings on Breton themes, inspired by
stained glass and the popular woodblock *Images d'Epinal*. Lacking
Gauguin's years of experience, Bernard also lacked his inhibitions,
and his experiments in simplification and caricatural drawing,
although proceeding along similar lines to Gauguin's, were much
51 bolder. In association with Louis Anquetin, for a year or so Bernard
had been painting portraits, still-lives and urban street scenes using
bold, flat or striated colour areas, surrounded by heavy black lines. In

66

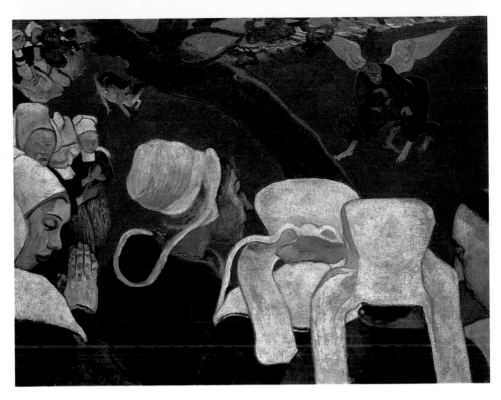

53 *La Vision après le Sermon. La Lutte de Jacob avec l'Ange* 1888

May 1888, reviewing a group of these works in *La Revue Indépendante*, Edouard Dujardin had dubbed the style 'cloisonnism', by association with the *cloisonné* technique in enamelling, whereby metal partitions or *cloisons* are used to divide one area of brightly coloured enamel from another. Gauguin, as we have seen, had already used a similar technique in his ceramics, and had been experimenting with flat colour areas in his most recent paintings. Bernard's example seems to have persuaded him that cloisonnism had some decorative advantages for painting too, particularly the increased brilliance it lent to the colours in the enclosed areas. But cloisonnism was never to play a particularly dominant role in Gauguin's painting. More importantly, the arrival of Bernard, who was a practising if somewhat wayward Christian, and his attractive and devout sister Madeleine, seems to have awakened Gauguin to the 54

54 *Madeleine Bernard* 1888

artistic inspiration to be found in Breton churches, calvaries and stained glass and to the potential of Breton piety as a pictorial theme to set against the despised 'Parisianism'. Increasingly, the curious pardons were being exploited as tourist attractions. At the same time, scholars of Breton life began to see signs of their being irreversibly modernized to bring them in line with Roman orthodoxy. In the hands of artists such as Jules Breton, Alphonse Leleux and Dagnan-Bouveret, Breton religious festivals were already a well-worked theme and when both Bernard and Gauguin turned out their crude, almost caricatural drawings and paintings of Breton women at prayer or in the fields that summer they were in a sense satirizing the seriousness of the Salon artists' attention to illusionistic realism. 32

In September 1888, Bernard painted an important canvas, *Les Bretonnes dans la prairie*, or *Pardon à Pont-Aven*, a bolder, more complex figure painting than any he had yet produced. The subject was based on the annual pardon that took place in Pont-Aven in September. Shortly afterwards, probably in response to witnessing the same pardon, Gauguin produced a composition of similar formal daring but greater literary complexity, which he entitled *La Vision après le Sermon. La Lutte de Jacob avec l'Ange*. 52 53

The art historical controversy surrounding the relationship between these two paintings has nearly obscured the fact that they were the fruits of a mutually beneficial working partnership that lasted for some two months. The collaborative links between Gauguin and Bernard embraced Charles Laval to some extent, and were keenly monitored by Vincent Van Gogh, who had engineered the encounter in the first place. The energy and excitement engendered by their joint experiments and discussions were expressed in the letters of both Gauguin and Bernard, letters in which, incidentally, Gauguin refers to 'le petit Bernard' and Bernard talks about Gauguin as 'le maître'. Gauguin chided Schuffenecker for his timidity and conservatism in contrast to young Bernard who 'feared nothing'; were Schuffenecker to come and join them in Pont-Aven, they would have someone to argue against in their heated discussions. They were 'tormenting Impressionism to death', as Gauguin put it, and the three of them were like 'tailleurs en peinture', by which he meant either stone-cutters or tailors, an analogy which presumably referred to the crudeness of their working methods or to the way their compositions resembled flat, coloured shapes pieced together.

55 *Vendanges à Arles. Misères humaines* 1888

56 *Autoportrait. Les Misérables* 1888

57 *Van Gogh peignant des soleils* 1888

47   As in the case of *Lutte Bretonne*, a parallel with the techniques of Japanese artists is clearly valid in the case of *La Vision*, with its asymmetrical composition, and its diagonal tree trunk separating the flattened upper and lower parts of the picture space. These biblical wrestlers, supposedly evoked in the minds of the praying women by the priest's sermon, have a synthetic, Japanese quality and may well have been derived from illustrations of wrestlers in Hokusai's celebrated *Mangwa* albums. Gauguin's stated plan of donating his painting to the local church, where its colour and simple shapes would rhyme with the stone pillars and stained glass, may also have had a bearing on the painting's decorative drama. He was not surprised, however, by the refusal of the two local priests he approached to accept his gift, and nor should we be. Gauguin had scarcely shown himself to be a member of the faithful and, quite apart from its unconventional and crude appearance, the painting was very much the product of a sceptical onlooker, projecting ideas such as 'rustic and superstitious simplicity' onto a group of worshippers, rather than an expression of orthodox devotional feeling. For all Gauguin's expressed anxiety to keep on good terms with the inhabitants of Pont-Aven and clear his debts with its traders, there is no evidence that they accepted or understood him, or that he succeeded in breaking through their natural mistrust of the outsider.

From the 1890s onwards, Bernard made public the claim that in embarking on *La Vision* Gauguin had changed his style beyond all recognition in response to his own bold example; moreover, he later accused Gauguin of taking for himself, and away from its true originator, all the credit for the new, revolutionary Synthetist style. It is undeniable that Gauguin and not Bernard came to be recognized as leader of the new avant-garde movement, but the justice of Bernard's claim is hard to establish, since both parties in the dispute were prone to take umbrage and, in their writings, to distort the facts to suit their own interests. Certainly, Bernard was not the only artist to fall foul of Gauguin's cavalier approach or to accuse him, rightly or wrongly, of piracy. By persuading Bernard to part with *Les Bretonnes dans la prairie* in exchange for one of his own works, and transporting it to Arles where it was copied by Vincent Van Gogh, Gauguin must have seemed to be making somewhat free with Bernard's discovery or, at the very least, acknowledging its usefulness to him. But when, in an unpublished article, Gauguin defended himself against Bernard's charge, he could speak from an unassailable position in pointing to the consistency of his own record as an artist, in contrast to Bernard's erratic stylistic progress after 1888.

Shortly before taking up the Van Goghs' invitation to go to Arles at the end of October, Gauguin sent Vincent a self-portrait. The latter 56 had requested his friends in Pont-Aven to paint one another's portraits and send them to him but in the event Gauguin, Bernard and Laval each found it easier to depict themselves. This was the first self-portrait Gauguin had produced since 1885, and the task seems to have intrigued him. Over the next year or two he turned again and again to his own image as a source of inspiration, as a motif for symbolic elaboration. In the accompanying letter to Vincent, he expounded the portrait's intended meaning, sensing that the underlying ideas surpassed the work itself. In so doing Gauguin tacitly accepted that Symbolist meanings might fail to function in the absence of a sympathetic exegesis (a danger that of course became increasingly acute in the twentieth century as artists' concepts were translated into more and more abstract forms). Gauguin inscribed his self-portrait *Les Misérables* and explained that his associating himself with Jean Valjean, the hounded and victimized hero of Victor Hugo's novel, was a way of symbolizing the plight of the Impressionist artist in contemporary society. Each element of the picture encoded a specific meaning: for example, the high colouring given to the flesh was meant to suggest the intense heat of the potter's kiln and thus the fires of creativity; the yellow floral background, like the wallpaper in a young girl's bedroom, signified the purity of the Impressionist, untainted by academicism. . . . This complexity was not entirely to Vincent Van Gogh's liking but the gist of the message Gauguin surely intended to convey was received loud and clear. The Van Gogh brothers hastened to assure him that by their good offices he would be cossetted, nurtured and restored to good health in Arles.

The extended anticipation of Gauguin's arrival in Arles had brought Vincent to a state of high nervous tension. He had long cherished the dream of setting up an artistic brotherhood and was most anxious that Gauguin should find the Yellow House to his liking. He had fitted it with the essentials for a shared existence, and decorated Gauguin's room with his own recent paintings. As Gauguin planned to stay for six months, he did not hesitate to make himself at home, immediately setting about reorganizing the kitchen,

30 *L'Arlésienne. Mme Ginoux* 1888

59 *Café de nuit à Arles* 1888

60 Vincent Van Gogh *The Night Café* 1888

ordering a new chest in which to store their belongings and an enormous roll of sackcloth on which to paint. He prided himself on his ability to run a more efficient household than Vincent, citing as evidence of his practical nature his years at sea. Everything suggested he intended to enjoy not having to foot the bill. Yet both artists were keen to impress on Theo, who was paying, the advantages of the new arrangement in terms of productivity.

In fact, it turned out to be a remarkably prolific period for them both. Gauguin, as Vincent had feared, was unimpressed by the landscape possibilities around Arles. The flat, treeless Camargue had none of the intimacy, variety and definition he had come to love in Brittany. Nor was he interested in the magnificent Roman remains. He turned his attention instead to the local women, an interest that developed naturally enough from his most recent Breton work. Partly thanks to Bizet's popular musical setting of Alphonse Daudet's drama, the Arlésiennes were famed throughout France for their spirit, beauty and dignity of bearing. In contrast to the Bretonnes, whose

starched, rounded and sometimes comical *coiffes* harked back to the middle ages, Gauguin found the women of Arles more sophisticated, reminiscent, with their black pleated shawls and elegant coiffure, of the virgins of ancient Greece, while at the same time suggesting a source of beautiful 'modern style'. Quite what he meant by this is hard to say. In his painting entitled *Café de nuit à Arles*, for which his portrait drawing *L'Arlésienne. Mme Ginoux*, in strong, simple controlled lines was the preparatory study, Gauguin uncharacteristically tackled a modern genre subject, even including such mundane details as the soda syphon and the prostitute's hair curlers. (Van Gogh painted the model at the same sitting, but preferred Gauguin's drawing to his own, later copying it.)

Although Gauguin probably treated this subject in order to demonstrate his misgivings about Vincent's earlier handling of the same theme, as he did on several occasions in Arles, he seems to have judged his *Café de nuit* as something of a false departure. On its completion, he turned to painting a grape harvesting scene, *Vendanges à Arles. Misères humaines*, working partly from memory and using considerably less deliberation. 'Too bad for exactitude', he jokingly wrote to Bernard, referring to the Breton figures he had included. Here, possibly for the first time, he worked directly onto coarse sackcloth instead of canvas. Describing the picture to Theo Van Gogh, he alluded to its exclusively male perspective which might shock potential buyers. This note throws light on the presumably sexual nature of the misery that afflicts the central seated figure, watched over by the woman identified by Gauguin as 'from Le Pouldu' in the traditional black hood of mourning, and points to a reason for the disarray of her clothing and the irregular absence of a *coiffe*. In Gauguin's view this was his most successful painting of 1888. Only subsequently have critics given greater prominence to *La Vision*. Gauguin made repeated use of that hunched, brooding figure in later works, usually retaining the meaning of sexual transgression or, more specifically, the fall of Eve.

In a later account of their work together, Gauguin claimed to have diverted Van Gogh away from his disorganized attempts at Neo-Impressionist arrangements of colour complementaries, which resulted in incomplete and monotonous harmonies, towards more clashing resonances, encouraging him to juxtapose strong, flat areas of colour as he himself was doing. He also persuaded Van Gogh to

76

follow him in undertaking compositions from memory, based on earlier sketches, away from the motif. The series of sunflower paintings, however, which Van Gogh executed during Gauguin's stay, were clearly done directly from the subject, as Gauguin's only 57 portrait of him shows. Possibly, in this series Van Gogh was emboldened by Gauguin's example to simplify his colour scheme but, if so, in reducing it almost to the single colour yellow he was venturing further in the direction of simplification than Gauguin. Besides, Vincent was hardly the compliant pupil Gauguin later suggested and was not to be shaken from his more firmly held convictions. In letters of early September they had established their essentially different attitudes to subject-matter. Whereas Van Gogh was forever in search of poetic motifs, Gauguin believed that poetry could be found in any subject and depended on the expressive manipulation of forms and colours. This essentially naturalist, formalist approach was a legacy of his years as an Impressionist but was no longer a strictly accurate account of more recent choice of and artful manipulation of subject-matter. The imaginative use of memory championed and demonstrated by Gauguin in his painting *Arlésiennes au jardin public, mistral* was essayed by Van Gogh in his 61, 62 parallel painting of the public gardens, *Memory of the Garden at Etten,* 63 into which he introduced memory images of his mother and sister in his home town of Etten. But Vincent quickly rejected this working method, to which he found himself temperamentally unsuited.

In a letter to Bernard of December 1888, written shortly after a visit they made by train to Montpellier, to see the Musée Fabre, Gauguin revealed considerable disagreement between himself and Van Gogh over the artists they most admired. Van Gogh tended towards the romantics and realists – Daumier, Daubigny, Ziem and Théodore Rousseau, 'all people I feel nothing for', Gauguin wrote, but he hated Ingres, Raphael, Degas, 'all people I admire'. Though enervating, these discussions with Vincent had the useful effect of clarifying in Gauguin's mind where his true stylistic allegiances now lay. The artists he admired, who all belonged within the classical tradition, were united by their calm, pondered, powerful drawing and their deliberate avoidance of chance effects, of slick or sloppy paint handling. Van Gogh, on the other hand, preferred those artists who expressed emotion through vigorous brushwork and colour. It is noticeable that Gauguin omitted Delacroix, realizing perhaps that to

61 *Arlésiennes* 1888

62 *Arlésiennes au jardin public, mistral* 1888

63 Vincent Van Gogh *Memory of the Garden at Etten* 1888

admit to their equal admiration of the great romantic would undermine the thesis he was constructing. Indeed, on a previous visit to Montpellier, Gauguin had made a copy of Delacroix's impressive portrait of *Aline la mulatresse*.

65, 66 Whether there was a reference to a figure from Delacroix's *Sardanapalus* in Gauguin's Arles painting *Dans les foins*, or yet another reminiscence of Degas, this erotic nude subject, based on fantasy, marked a new departure for Gauguin and a sharp divergence from
64 Van Gogh's subject-matter. *Ondine* or *Dans les Vagues*, a somewhat similar fantasy image of an abandoned nude woman seen from behind, again reminiscent of the nudes of Degas, can now be ascribed to Gauguin's Arles period. Although it bears the date 1889, it appears
67 in reverse in the background of his Arles self-portrait. Painted on the same coarse sackcloth he had purchased while there, and referred to by Van Gogh in a letter, this self-portrait was one of the last pictures Gauguin made in Arles, perhaps intending it as a companion piece to
57 and contrast with his portrait *Van Gogh peignant des soleils*. By his inclusion of a recently worked, highly synthetic image within the

78

64 *Ondine* 1889 (see *Ill. 67*, painted against a reversed detail of this picture)

65 *Dans les foins. En pleine chaleur* 1888

66 Eugène Delacroix *The Death of Sardanapalus* (detail) 1827

self-image, Gauguin established a format for self-portraiture which he repeated on several later occasions.

After dispatching a consignment of five recent canvases to Theo, word got back to Gauguin from Paris that Degas had seen them and, with the exception of *Vendanges à Arles* which he could not fathom, had enthusiastically admired them. Theo may also have passed on reports of Degas's envious interest in the energetic working relationship Gauguin and Van Gogh seemed to have established together, so different from his own feelings of incapacity. Once again, however, it was to be a short-lived collaboration. Both artists were beginning to realize by late 1888 that such a charged atmosphere could not be sustained without a catastrophe; the break came on 23 December when, after a drunken argument, in an inflamed state, Vincent lunged at Gauguin with a razor. Gauguin fled and discovered the next morning that in remorse Vincent had turned the blade on himself, slicing off a part of his ear. Having ascertained that his companion's life was not in danger, Gauguin removed himself from the scene and returned hastily to Paris, cutting short his stay in Provence by some four months.

Although the experiment of working with Van Gogh was ultimately disastrous, once the memory of this violent incident had receded, there was no reason for either artist to feel it had been a wasted or negative period in their careers. Gauguin had turned out a varied group of paintings, mostly of high calibre. In conversation he and Van Gogh had touched on many vital topics; together they had reviewed their positions in the light of the history of art; Gauguin's talk of the tropics had inspired Vincent's enthusiasm, making the plan to return there seem a more reasonable and tangible one, one worth working towards. On returning to Brittany in spring 1889, Gauguin found his response to its character had gained new focus and purpose now that he was able to contrast it with the south, and many of the projects for picture-making which he followed through in 1889 stemmed from the discussions that had taken place in Arles.

67 *Autoportrait* 1888 (see *Ill. 64*)

68 *Nature morte à l'estampe japonaise* 1889

CHAPTER FOUR

Leader of the Symbolists (1889–1891)

Lodged once again in Paris with the Schuffeneckers, Gauguin seems to have lost no time in resuming the work he had left in abeyance the previous winter and renewing contacts with the artistic and social world. Just two days after his arrival, he attended the public execution by guillotine of a celebrated murderer, Prado, an experience he later recalled in his autobiographical writings. Although there was nothing exceptional about attending executions in Paris at this date, in view of Gauguin's own recent brush with death the event must have had a particular poignancy. There is every reason to connect it with the strange ceramic *Self-Portrait Jug* he made in Chaplet's new studio   89, 68
early in 1889, with its closed eyes and pooling of red-stained *flambé* glaze round the apparently severed neck. Here, once again, Gauguin played on the image of the artist as society's pariah and victim.

    Given Degas's recent expressions of interest and support, it is quite possible that Gauguin took the opportunity of visiting the elder artist in his studio. Such a visit would explain the continuing vestiges of Degas's influence in his paintings of early 1889. In Degas's studio Gauguin might well have seen the artist's copy of Holbein's *Anne of Cleves*, the painting that has often been seen as the source of Gauguin's portrait of the inn-keeper's wife in Pont-Aven, *La Belle Angèle.*   72
Portrait de Mme Satre. He would also have been exposed to Degas's recent pastel studies of the nude, all the more relevant to Gauguin's current preoccupation with the nude theme. In the important canvas entitled *Femmes se baignant. La vie et la mort*, for instance, which   71
developed conceptually from the paintings Gauguin had done in Arles, the right-hand figure seems to bear a general resemblance to Degas's women bathers. The left-hand figure, though, who symbolizes death, came from a very different source (as Wayne Anderson was the first to demonstrate): it indicates Gauguin beginning to venture beyond the Louvre and the art galleries, and to explore the lesser known corners of Paris, notably the newly formed collections of folkloric, 'primitive' and ethnographical items, many

69 Peruvian mummy from the northern Andes, 1100–1400
70 *Eve. Pas écouter li li menteur* 1889

of which had been gathered on recent archaeological and colonial expeditions. Gauguin based the pose of his death figure on the almost foetal pose of a Peruvian mummy, a somewhat gruesome exhibit at the Ethnographical Museum in the Trocadéro Palace. A borrowing from such an unlikely, non-European source contradicted Gauguin's indebtedness to Degas, as he was not slow to realize. Writing to Schuffenecker in the summer of 1889, he expressed growing misgivings about the naturalism of Degas, arguing that his dispassionate observations carried the 'smell of the model' and lacked a sense of mystery. By so deliberately giving his own nudes titles that suggest their symbolic or allegorical significance, Gauguin was surely trying to distance himself from what Degas had achieved.

The nude was traditionally a vehicle for allegorical presentation. The portrait, however, was a genre in which the artist was still expected to produce a recognizable likeness, and not take too many liberties. Gauguin's interest in portraiture had been greatly stimulated by the example of Vincent Van Gogh, for whom it was unquestionably the noblest genre. When Gauguin turned to the new

69

86

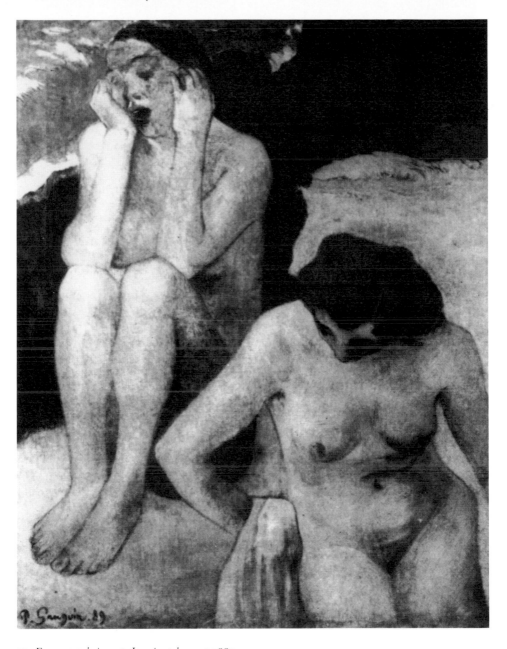

71 *Femmes se baignant. La vie et la mort* 1889

LA BELLE ANGÈLE

P Gauguin 89

72 *La Belle Angèle. Portrait de Mme Satre* 1889

73 *La Famille Schuffenecker* 1889

problem of a group portrait of the Schuffenecker family, early in
1889, perhaps as a gesture of recompense for their generous
hospitality, he did not hesitate to inject it with his own personal
feelings and meanings, with the result that he was in danger of
alienating the sitters. He had frequently referred to Mme
Schuffenecker as a shrew, and he represented her here as a
threatening, almost predatory figure with a claw-like hand, her bulky
presence accentuating the cringing, self-effacing stance of Schuffenecker himself. Although we have no record of the latter's reaction, in
his anxiety to make a name as a serious painter he cannot have been
too pleased to see the tribulations of his private life demonstrated in
this way. We only know that the painting was not exhibited publicly
during Gauguin's lifetime. On the other hand, we do know
something about Mme Satre's reaction when faced with Gauguin's

73

74 *Autoportrait au Christ jaune* 1889

highly stylized portrayal. Reputed in Pont-Aven as a beauty, she was
so insulted by the somewhat cow-like rendering that she threw the
portrait back in Gauguin's face. It remained unsold until 1891 when
Degas acquired it for 450 francs. Henceforth Gauguin's more
extravagant experiments in symbolic portraiture were confined to his
own self-image.

For Gauguin, 1889 was to be a year for testing the public's response
to the important advances he had made. He knew that only a public
success would prove him in the eyes of his wife, with whom he had
had strained and infrequent contact over the previous year. She
continued, nevertheless, to dominate his thoughts and to provide a
spur to his ambitions. Seven of his recent works went on show in

February at the exhibition of the Vingt group in Brussels, an occasion on which several of the paintings received their full poetic titles, among them *La Vision après le Sermon. La Lutte de Jacob avec l'Ange* and *Vendanges à Arles. Misères humaines*. The critical response was disappointing, perhaps because the critics, only just attuned to the Neo-Impressionists, were unprepared for Gauguin's 'abstractions' from nature and his un-naturalistic colours. For the most part, they treated his Symbolist pretensions with derision and *La Vision* in particular was much mocked. In the Paris weekly *La Cravache*, however, Gauguin was congratulated by Octave Maus, secretary to the Vingt group, on the 'primitive character of his paintings' and on the charm and refinement of his colour harmonies; Maus applauded Gauguin for leaving behind his debt to the landscape Impressionists and deemed the admiration of Degas ample compensation for the incomprehension of the public.

Gauguin's absence from any group exhibition in Paris since 1886 made him very conscious of the need to be seen there again, preferably in the context of works by other artists working along parallel lines with himself. Although 1889 had opened with a slump on the stock market, Paris was in a fever of preparation for the grandest Universal Exhibition yet, which would celebrate the centenary of the French Revolution in an orgy of commercialism from May to October. Art would of course have its place in the exhibition, next to France's technological achievements, and a huge Palais des Beaux-Arts was erected on the Champ de Mars site, under the shadow of the newly constructed Eiffel Tower. But as was to be expected, only officially sanctioned artists were to participate. The 'Decennial Exhibition', which was intended to give foreign visitors an insight into French art of the last decade, was dominated by the stars of the Salon, such as Bouguereau, Carolus-Duran, Bastien-Lepage and Dagnan-Bouveret. A few of the earliest examples of Impressionism were allowed into the 'Centennial' but the Monets, Renoirs and Pissarros occupied a very small enclave amid the rooms full of French history painting. Seurat and his Neo-Impressionist group would make their presence felt at the annual show of the Indépendants in September, which, with the influx of tourists, was fairly certain to increase its audience.

Both Gauguin and Schuffenecker saw the Universal Exhibition as an opportunity to make a big noise for themselves; it would be a

P Gauguin

75 *Bretonnes à la barrière* 1889

sensational *coup* to get their works shown inside the designated exhibition ground. They achieved their end by persuading M Volpini, the director of one of the larger exhibition cafés, the Café des Arts, to hang their pictures on his walls. Theo Van Gogh was not in favour of this plan, seeing it as a vulgar backstage manœuvre, and he advised Vincent not to have any part in the show. Guillaumin also turned down the invitation to participate. A group of a hundred or more works was eventually mustered, by Gauguin, Bernard, Schuffenecker, Laval, Anquetin and some younger, lesser-known artists, among them Daniel de Monfreid (a friend of Schuffenecker's, who was later a devoted correspondent and mediator when Gauguin was in Tahiti). The exhibition lasted from May to July and a small, hand-printed catalogue was produced by the artists.

92

Paul Gauguin
Les Cigales et les fourmis

76 *Les Cigales et les fourmis* 1889

Hoping to make some fast money through the sale of lithographs, Gauguin and Bernard had compiled albums of *Bretonneries* using bold, simplified designs, printing them from zinc, which was a cheaper surface than stone. For this first venture into printmaking, Gauguin mainly used subjects from his Breton and Martinique 75 paintings of the previous two years. However, his growing appetite for suggesting oblique and mysterious meanings led to his retrospectively loading some of the images with literary titles and, as in the case of some of his paintings, there was a danger of these sounding pretentious or superfluous. Without its title, the image in *Les Cigales et les fourmis* can be read on a straightforward level as an 76 observation of daily life in Martinique. With its reference to La Fontaine's fable, the title adds a second level of literary meaning, or perhaps of ambiguity: which are the grasshoppers, which the ants? The paintings Gauguin showed included most of those already exhibited in Brussels, with the notable exception of *La Vision*, and a few new works such as *Eve* and *Ondine (Dans les Vagues)*. The two latter images were combined to form the frontispiece to the exhibition catalogue.

70

77

Gauguin's hope, as he candidly explained to Theo Van Gogh, was that this show would demonstrate to the older Impressionists and to Seurat that he was now a free artist, able to summon support from other quarters than theirs and able to command public and critical attention in his own right. One critic whose support Gauguin actively cultivated was the young Symbolist poet Albert Aurier, a friend of Emile Bernard's. In April 1889 Aurier launched a new, light-hearted and risqué weekly journal, *Le Moderniste*, addressed to an urbane male readership. This publication featured not only the Volpini exhibition at the Café des Arts, illustrating some of the works on show there, but it also gave Bernard and Gauguin space to try their hand at art criticism. As a result, almost all the summer issues of the short-lived periodical sounded the drum for the new Pont-Aven Synthetist style, thus making the declared editorial policy of eclecticism and impartiality sound rather hollow. Other reviewers were less comprehending, notably Jules Antoine in *Art et Critique*, who complained of the barbarousness of the works on show and of the difficulty of telling which artists were Impressionists and which Synthetists. Of much greater weight was the review in *La Cravache* by Félix Fénéon, who argued that Gauguin, in this exhibition, had shown himself to be, like Seurat, a defector from Impressionism. All along, but by different means, so Fénéon argued, Gauguin had been working towards a similar goal to Seurat, an art of 'synthesis and premeditation'. As though arming himself against future attacks, Gauguin copied and treasured the opening paragraph of this review, in which his most recent canvases were said to crown and confirm the consistent tendency of his paintings, sculptures and ceramics towards archaism and exoticism. He was less enamoured of Fénéon's suggestion that Anquetin, whom both he and Fénéon considered an artist of inferior talent, might have had some influence on his style. However, Gauguin's protestation that he did not know Anquetin was scarcely proof that there had been no cross-fertilization: Bernard had effectively acted as mediator between the two artists. Possibly

94

EXPOSANTS

Paul Gauguin	E. Schuffenecker	Emile Bernard
Charles Laval	Louis Anquetin	Louis Roy
Léon Fauché	Georges Daniel	Ludovic Nemo

77 *Aux Roches noires*, frontispiece of the Volpini exhibition catalogue, 1889

Gauguin sensed the double-edged nature of Fénéon's observation that both Bernard and Laval would need to free themselves from the stamp of Gauguin, whose work was 'too arbitrary or at least results from a state of mind that is too peculiar for newcomers usefully to be able to take him as their starting point'. Fénéon clearly did not think that Gauguin had the potential to lead others, as Seurat had done, or had established a style on which others could build.

Although to our eyes the paintings exhibited at the Volpini Café des Arts scarcely form a coherent, homogeneous group, there was some consensus of critical opinion about their appearance. Whether damning or praising the fact that the new pictures were quirky, arbitrary and personal, most critics commented on the daringly simple, childlike and caricatural drawing and the flagrantly flat, anti-illusionistic colour application. These innovations had the effect of exciting and intriguing a whole section of disaffected young art students, already rebelling against the outworn academic dictates of their teachers (whose sole ideal seemed to be illusionistic trickery), but who had been unsure how to proceed towards a more 'honest' form of art. Isolated individuals such as the southerner Aristide Maillol and the Dutchman Jan Verkade were fired by what they saw at the Volpini exhibition, but the key figures in this band of potential

disciples were the students at the Académie Julian, well-educated
young artists of a more intellectual bent than Gauguin, notably Paul
Sérusier and Maurice Denis. With a group of like-minded friends,
these students had already formed a secret artistic fraternity within the
art school, half-jokingly calling themselves the 'Nabis', Hebrew for
prophets. By visiting Theo Van Gogh's gallery they had familiarized
themselves with the recent Synthetist works of Gauguin, the raw
elements of which Sérusier had gleaned in Pont-Aven in October
1888. On returning to Paris at the beginning of the new term, Sérusier
had brought with him *Le Talisman, le bois d'amour*, an embryonic
abstract landscape done under Gauguin's instructions. Gauguin, and
Sérusier in his wake, used it as an object lesson in how to paint with
pure colour, straight from the tube, without adhering too closely to
the details or local colour of the scene to be represented. The idea of
disseminating revolution in one of the strongholds of artistic
conservatism greatly amused Gauguin and as a politician he could also

78

see its practical advantages. So when Sérusier wrote to Gauguin, after seeing the Volpini show, 'I am one of yours', and announced his intention of coming to join Gauguin in Brittany, he was warmly welcomed. The practical efforts Sérusier and Denis made to support Gauguin over the next year or so, for example by publishing a combative article entitled 'Définition du Néo-Traditionnisme' in August 1890, penned by Denis but in many ways a joint undertaking, also received the artist's appreciative approval.

Gauguin was a firm believer in artists taking up their own defence, arguing their case. In July 1889, in two consecutive articles in *Le Moderniste*, he aired his own observations about the Universal Exhibition. He complained of the paucity of modern design to be seen there, and pointed out the need for a new kind of ornament to suit iron, the building material of the age. He contrasted the wonderful design and craftsmanship of the middle ages with the lifelessness of present-day furniture and sculpture. His cry for authenticity, truth to materials, had a particular bearing on his own work as a wood-carver and ceramicist but also showed that he was in tune with the growing European-wide movement promoting the traditional arts and crafts. He singled out from the mass of Sèvres and other manufactured pots on show the exceptional work of Chaplet and Delaherche. (Lest any readers of the article should fail to make the connection, Aurier appended a note demanding to know why Gauguin's own remarkable pots and statuettes were nowhere to be seen at the Exhibition!) Gauguin had few words of praise for the fine art on show. He pointed out that the absence of a representative work by Manet in a public collection was a public disgrace. Here also he joined his voice to a contemporary campaign, launched by Monet earlier in the year, to get Manet's *Olympia* bought for the nation and installed in the state's collection of modern art, the Luxembourg.

For most people the Universal Exhibition provided an array of ephemeral distractions but for some it offered more lasting food for thought. Although drawn to the coloured fountains and the Javanese dancers, Camille Pissarro was repelled by the underlying French ideology, with all its nationalistic, materialistic and imperialistic fervour. Gauguin was a less critical visitor. He went repeatedly to watch the stunts of Buffalo Bill, a reflection of the unashamedly macho side of his character, which also emerged in his enjoyment of fencing and boxing. He was a curious and assiduous visitor of the

79 The Palais des Colonies at the Universal
Exhibition 1889, Paris

80 Page of studies of figures in costume at
the Universal Exhibition (Annamites and Arabs),
1889?

79   Colonial Exhibition too, which demonstrated aspects of the life and
culture of French-held territories such as Madagascar, Martinique,
Tahiti and Tonkin (now Vietnam).

    Gauguin's apparently naïve acceptance and Pissarro's criticism of
the interests behind the Exhibition are a fair indication of the
divergent political views of the two artists. Certainly, reactionary
political concerns had governed the organization of the Exhibition. If
an especially important place was given to the delegation from
Tonkin, annexed from China in a recent and bloody conflict, it was
undoubtedly to persuade the government's critics of the worthy gain
that had been made and to attract potential colonists. The message of
the Exhibition was directed not only at the French voters, so recently
and dangerously swayed by the absolutist claims of General
Boulanger; it was also aimed at those new and far-flung subjects,
chosen to come to Paris for a few months as living exhibits of their
native countries. Indeed, E. Monod, reckoning up the score at the end

98

of this exhibition year, confidently reassured his readers that the message had been got across: 'our natives took away the impression that France is a rich and powerful country, whose moral superiority they recognize and whose authority they will be less and less tempted to contest'.

Although Gauguin would scarcely have endorsed these sentiments, his appetite for the colonial life was unquestionably reawakened at the Universal Exhibition by the spectacle of the colourful native costumes, dwellings and exotic artefacts – a huge Tonkinese Buddha, 80 for example – and encounters with different racial groups, some of whom he sketched. His ideas, repeated over the coming months, of how easily life could be lived in, say, Madagascar or Tahiti, reflected the information provided in the official handouts. At first, his plans for returning to the tropics focused on Tonkin. Perhaps, like the gossip journalists, he was disappointed by the ugliness of the delegation of Tahitian women, whose legendary beauty had been praised so evocatively by Pierre Loti a decade earlier in his novel *Rarahu* or *Le Marriage de Loti*. Evidently, the colonial functionary responsible for selecting them had been more concerned with their morals than their looks, the two reputedly never going together in Tahiti. Like the gossip columnists, Gauguin became obsessed by the dream of tropical idylls, and he was prompted to formulate his artistic image of primitive beauty, a new ideal to set against the lifeless ideal

81   woman of Europe. In *La Femme noire*, for instance, a ceramic sculpture probably modelled in May 1889, the image of the black woman was calculated to disturb spectators. He was particularly keen for Theo Van Gogh to put it on show in July, on its completion, before the Universal Exhibition closed.

So it was with his thoughts firmly set on the tropics that Gauguin returned once more to Brittany in June. No sooner had he arrived than he complained of how crowded and spoilt Pont-Aven had become. He decided to move some fifteen kilometres away to the more remote hamlet of Le Pouldu, where he had worked briefly the previous year. Set on a rocky peninsula, Le Pouldu was characterized by scattered farms, windswept dunes and sandy beaches. Gauguin was joined at the Hôtel des Grandes Sables by two new disciples, Paul Sérusier and a wealth Dutchman, Meyer de Haan, to whom he had been introduced by Theo Van Gogh. At first, Sérusier feared that Gauguin was just a joker, not the serious philosophical artist for whom he was searching. Both Sérusier and De Haan had a strong philosophical bent, to which Gauguin made reference in his symbolic

83   portrait of De Haan entitled *Nirvana*. They no doubt helped to keep Gauguin abreast of the latest anti-positivist thinking that was becoming fashionable in intellectual circles in Paris. If De Haan's reading included Milton and Carlyle, as another of Gauguin's paintings indicates, Sérusier was reading Edmond Schuré's *Les Grands Initiés*, a comparative study of world religions, in which Christianity was given a logical but by no means more prominent place beside Buddhism and the Indian Vedic religions. A number of Gauguin's more abstruse images from this date onwards suggests at least a passing familiarity with these esoteric strands of Symbolist discourse.

On a more practical level, Sérusier, working under Gauguin's tutelage, quickly overcame his initial mistrust but was perplexed by the problem of whether or not to paint from nature, how much art depended on observation, how much on memory and imagination.

82 *Eve exotique* 1890

One senses that he was impatient to throw off, there and then, the academic yoke of copying, but nervous about doing so, whereas Gauguin, who had the capacity and experience to take a longer look at his artistic progress, was aware that a period spent in fairly straightforward contact with nature was a necessary prelude if he was to launch and sustain another concerted effort at symbolic abstraction. After the experience of Arles, Gauguin felt especially drawn to the harsher, more primitive aspects of the Breton landscape. In a letter of October to Vincent Van Gogh he wrote that the very costumes of the peasants seemed to express the sadness and god-fearing rigour of their lives. He contented himself with fairly naturalistic renderings of landscape motifs in the immediate vicinity, 84 often working with De Haan or Sérusier, paying a new attention to agricultural activities, perhaps another sign of Vincent's influence.

Working on landscapes or still-lives had the advantage of allowing them to concentrate on technical problems, in Gauguin's case, how best to achieve the even, matt, rustic and primitive appearance he wanted in his pictures. Works such as *Misères humaines* had shown him how extremely coarse canvas could be used to absorb much of the greasy base of oil paint, leaving only a thin opaque coat of colour. He also experimented with a technique involving wet newspaper, paste and the application of hot irons – a technique learnt from a picture restorer – to produce an unvariegated matt surface.

Gauguin later described the general goals he had been working towards: 'I scrutinized the horizons, seeking that harmony of human 85 life with animal and vegetable life through compositions in which I allowed the great voice of the earth to play an important part.' In 87 works such as *Moisson en Bretagne*, it is the strength of the underlying design rather than the colour or brushwork that establishes harmony: lines are smoothed and simplified and strong rhythms established through repeated shapes (the tree and the shaggy green bush echo the shape of the heads of the oxen in the foreground); colour is applied flatly and in an unemphatic way. Much the same technique was used 86 in the large composition *Ramasseuses de varech*, also painted at Le Pouldu. Seaweed had regularly been gathered there for use by farmers as a fertilizer, but in the nineteenth century it was also an important source of iodine. Gauguin, in common with many of his contemporaries, seems to have been struck by the melancholy aspect of this strange form of harvest.

83 *Nirvana. Portrait de Meyer de Haan* 1889

84 Jacob Meyer de Haan *Farmyard at Le Pouldu* 1889

85 *Rentrée des vaches à Pont-Aven* 1889?

86 *Ramasseuses de varech* 1889

87 *Moisson en Bretagne* 1889

88 *Soyez amoureuses et vous serez heureuses* 1889

89 *Self-Portrait Jug*, 1889

90 *Le Christ jaune* 1889

91 Crucifix from the chapel at Le Trémalo, near Pont-Aven
92 Study for *Le Christ jaune* 1889

Although these works were by no means naturalistic transcriptions
90   of the surrounding landscape, with *Le Christ jaune* Gauguin
consciously embarked on a more imaginative and ambitious series of
works, once again inspired by Breton piety. The figure of Christ was
91, 92 based on Gauguin's simplified sketch of a wooden crucifix in the
ancient chapel of Trémalo near Pont-Aven. The synthetic
interpretation of the original carving was carried through into the
painting. The flat, unmodelled and unvariegated yellow, Gauguin
later explained, was intended to express the feelings he had about the
desolate isolation and medieval quality of Breton life, though in all
probability the yellowish stain of the crucifix itself first suggested the
use of this colour. He evidently used the technique of blotting the
surface with wet newspaper as the print is still visible on the paint
surface, perhaps to dull the glossiness of the oil pigment and give an
aged appearance to that strident yellow. Quite possibly the idea
95   behind this subject, and *Le Christ vert. Le Calvaire Breton* which

108

93 Yann D'Argent *Le Calvaire de Quillinen près de Quimper* 1893
94 Deposition from the calvary at Nizon, near Pont-Aven

followed, can be traced to a poem by Marie Krysinska, *Le Calvaire*, published in *La Revue Indépendante* in June 1889. Written in free verse by one of the alleged pioneers of this revolutionary form in Symbolist poetry, the poem describes a simple stone calvary representing the Christ of sorrows which seems to the poet to link symbolically the desolate heath and its earthbound penitents with the 'glorious golden sky' above.

The visual source for *Le Christ vert* was the carved stone pieta in the village of Nizon near Pont-Aven. The calvaries were notable and distinct features of the Breton scene for the visitor and it is surprising that until then Gauguin, with his sculptural interests, had made no reference to them. His desire to avoid the well-established conventions for painting Brittany, conventions exemplified by the slightly later calvary painting of the Breton Salon artist Yann D'Argent, *Le Calvaire de Quillinen près de Quimper* (1893), may have blinded him to their expressive potential. Although essentially the

94

93

95 Le Christ vert. Le Calvaire Breton 1889

96 *Le Christ au Jardin des Olives* 1889

local inspiration and message of workaday piety of the two paintings were the same, where D'Argent gave a realistic sense of scale and location, Gauguin deliberately distorted the various elements, severing the deposition motif from the rest of the calvary, making the carved figures life-size and merging them with the landscape, using not the close setting of Nizon but instead the dune-scape of Le Pouldu, more dramatic and expressive of the mood of sadness he wished to convey.

It seems as though Gauguin's responsiveness to local Breton art, in the form of sculpture and traditional carved furniture, had lain dormant until he moved to Le Pouldu. In 1888 he had got as far as sketching a carved 'armoire' along traditional Breton lines, using his own quirky and rather frivolous motifs, but in the autumn of 1889, 97

97 Design for the decoration of a bookcase, 1888

98 Breton *lit clos* (box bed)

after first modelling the design in clay, he embarked on his most ambitious wood carving to date, *Soyez amoureuses et vous serez heureuses*, using a panel of fine linden wood, especially ordered through Schuffenecker from Paris. Wooden panels, sometimes carved with figures and inscriptions, were used as sliding doors in the traditional Breton box beds and although Gauguin's panel seems not to have been intended for such a function, it may owe part of its inspiration and imagery to such indigenous carvings. Indeed, the Trémalo chapel where Gauguin found the crucifix for *Le Christ jaune* boasted beams and lintels carved with painted human and animal heads. Some of the details in his complex design bear a resemblance to such grotesques. The male figure attempting to seduce the naked woman with negroid features, whose wedding ring is emphasized, is yet another self-portrait. What personal experience, if any, this conjunction may refer to has never emerged from the wealth of speculation about Gauguin's private life. For all its deliberately primitive appearance, the message Gauguin evidently wanted his carving to convey was a modern, secular and cynical one, an ironic reflection on the hollowness of the motto 'Be in love and you will be happy'. *Soyez amoureuses* was in a sense a labour of love, carved over many weeks during spare intervals from painting, the contours of the woman's body painstakingly smoothed, stained and polished in contrast to the more roughly hewn areas where the cuts of the chisel were deliberately left visible.

Gauguin had invested much time and energy in this carving and in his new religious canvases and was clearly upset when reports of their negative reception filtered back from Paris. To assist Theo Van Gogh, he wrote elaborate, though still open-ended explanations of their meanings, but he expressed his impatience of people's desire to pin him down: 'either it's good or it's not artistic'. Ironically, Gauguin's feelings were echoed two years later by the critic P. M. Olin, reviewing *Soyez amoureuses* at the Vingt show in Brussels. He found fault with the inscription on the grounds of its over-precise fixing of meaning which, he felt, removed the suggestive quality of the imagery and made the work into a sort of rebus or picture puzzle.

In view of the consternation his works were evidently causing in Paris in the late autumn of 1889, Gauguin decided to hold back the one picture that he was certain would be misconstrued, *Le Christ au Jardin des Olives*, though he sent a sketch and description of it to

99 Letter to Vincent Van Gogh, November 1889, with sketches of *Soyez amoureuses* and *Le Christ au Jardin des Olives*

Vincent Van Gogh. Much has been made of the blasphemous implications of Gauguin's identification with Christ, for it is fairly clear, despite the brilliant red hair, that he used his own features for the face; moreover, Gauguin at this time frequently compared his own trials with those of Christ. Vincent was distressed by the work, and strongly disapproved of the entirely imaginary turn Gauguin's and Bernard's imagery seemed to be taking, arguing that if *he* were to attempt to convey the message of Christ's sorrow, he would make a painting of olive groves, something he could actually see.

100 *Bonjour M Gauguin* 1889

101 Portrait charge de Gauguin
1889

102 (OPPOSITE) Marc-Antoine
Verdier *Le Christ couronné
d'épines. Portrait d'Alfred Bruyas*
c. 1850

103 Interior of the dining
room at the inn of Marie
Henry at Le Pouldu, with
murals by Gauguin and
Meyer de Haan

It is worth noting that Gauguin and Bernard were not alone in using the image of the calvary or of Christ's agony in an autobiographical way. In 1886 Octave Mirbeau had published his novel *Le Calvaire*, transparently based on the author's sufferings at the hands of a faithless mistress, and Albert Aurier's poem *La Montagne du Doute*, first published in 1889 and well known to Bernard and Gauguin, equated the burden borne by Christ with that of the poet, endowed with the dubious gift of genius. Much of the responsibility for enabling such parallels to be made lay with Ernest Renan, whose *Vie de Jésus* of 1866 had brought a modern, positivist and psychological approach to bear on the known facts of Jesus's life on earth, effectively explaining Christ's sufferings as though he were an ordinary mortal. After falling out with Gauguin in 1891, Bernard condemned his former comrade's shallow understanding of Christianity: 'Look at Gauguin's Christs, they are human, they are of this world. . . . Christ did not shed stupid tears onto beautiful veined hands. All that has to do with Gauguin, that's to say with self-adoration, with the purely profane, with Renan.'

116

104 *Portrait de femme à la nature morte de Cézanne* 1890

105 *La Perte de pucelage* 1890

Gauguin might well have had a visual precedent in mind when he embarked on this symbolic self-portrait. On his visit to Montpellier with Vincent Van Gogh, both artists had been struck by the many portraits made by notable contemporary artists of Alfred Bruyas, the enlightened but somewhat narcissistic patron whose collection dominated the Musée Fabre there. One of these, by Marc-Antoine Verdier, portrayed him as *Le Christ couronné d'épines*, whose   102 colouring and general disposition has similarities with Gauguin's.

Among the decorations Gauguin and his friends painted onto the   103 walls and doors of the dining room in Marie Henry's inn at Le Pouldu, were two further highly contrived self-portraits by Gauguin. In one of them, essentially a caricature, he used a totally flat, linear   101 style, as on a playing card, to present himself symbolically as the Fallen Angel. In the second, *Bonjour M Gauguin*, Gauguin alluded to   100 the title at least of Courbet's *Bonjour M Courbet*, which represents Bruyas in a landscape setting greeting his celebrated artistic protégé Courbet, who is dressed in the guise of the Wandering Jew. Although Courbet too had drawn the analogy between the artist and the outcast, he nevertheless represented himself as boldly squaring up to his patron, whereas Gauguin's depiction of a chance encounter with a Breton peasant woman merely reinforced his isolation and alienation. In all these paintings, Gauguin seems to have been concerned to convey a predominant mood of depression and suffering, tinged by a world-weary cynicism; in a long letter to Theo Van Gogh, he asserted that in his recent works he had sought to suggest the idea of suffering without explaining what sort of suffering. This claim in itself demands some explanation, for Gauguin's aims sometimes appear contradictory. At one level he was undoubtedly wary of being judged a 'literary' painter and sought to dissociate himself from the notion of producing works of art that had to be 'read' to be understood. Yet at another he deliberately cultivated complex, ambiguous and autobiographical meaning, almost as a gesture of defiance: if the critics were so woefully unable to appreciate him, then he would make sure they could not understand him either. In June 1890 he wrote to Vincent Van Gogh, for the last time as it turned out, 'Alas I see myself condemned to be less and less understood, and I must resign myself to following my path alone, dragging out an existence without family, like a pariah. . . . The savage will return to the wilderness.'

In the context of Symbolism, which demanded that artists should touch the spectator's feelings through the combination of forms and colours, not through sentimental stories, and should suggest and evoke abstract ideas rather than explain and document reality, Gauguin's confused aspirations find some sort of rationale. Increasingly, he was directing his creative products at a select Symbolist audience, accepting that the masses would have to be rebuffed along the way. Because his recent works had met with only muted enthusiasm from Theo Van Gogh, at the end of 1889 Gauguin's confidence needed bolstering and he appealed to Schuffenecker and Bernard for their opinions. Evidently he received satisfaction from those quarters but the flattering exchanges between him and Bernard during the first half of 1890 soon began to sound somewhat hollow. Bernard's own progress had been far from straightforward since 1888, and their artistic paths were beginning to diverge. Like Gauguin, he had spent time in Brittany in 1889 and had worked on religious motifs inspired by primitive woodcuts, but since visiting various exhibitions and museums in Paris self-doubts had set in, and he was flung hither and thither by uncertainties as to his talents and direction as an artist. In addition, he was suffering from family difficulties and an unhappy love affair so that, by the summer of 1890, he was ready to abandon the attempt to make ends meet as an artist in Europe and to take up Gauguin's invitation to accompany him to his current tropical destination, Madagascar. But Bernard's resolve in this or any such undertaking was shaky, as Gauguin was well aware. For one thing, it hinged on the outcome of a proposed business deal worth 5000 francs with a wealthy inventor, a certain Docteur Charlopin. For this investment Charlopin would receive a bulk consignment of pictures by each artist at bargain prices which he would then retail.

If Bernard's loyalty was an unknown quantity, Gauguin now had, in addition to De Haan and Sérusier, a growing number of new disciples in Brittany, including Séguin, Filiger, the Danes Ballin and Willumsen, the Dutchman Verkade and the Pole Slewinski. Many of these artists had come to Paris for the Universal Exhibition and been drawn to Brittany by the revelation of seeing the works at the Volpini show. Their contact with Gauguin himself was often of short duration, but the Pont-Aven aesthetic had now taken root and could be expected to survive without him. The flattering distraction of so

106 Paul Cézanne *Nature morte, compotier, verre et pommes c.* 1880

many younger talents looking to him as a figurehead undoubtedly swelled Gauguin's ego, but it did nothing to alleviate the difficulties of finding buyers for his recent work.

The fact that he was principally occupied by the ways and means of earning his passage overseas and securing a post in the colonies meant that Gauguin's output of paintings, normally substantial, fell off sharply in 1890. In anticipation of the work to come, which, he promised Theo Van Gogh, would be grander and more complete than anything he had yet done, Gauguin allowed himself to abandon his canvases, seeking to conserve his resources and energies. A few landscapes done 'mechanically' from nature at Le Pouldu date from this year and an unusually direct, solidly modelled portrait of a Breton woman, Marie Lagadu, in which the figure is set against the background of the Cézanne *Nature morte, compotier, verre et pommes,* which Gauguin still owned. The presence and purpose of so obvious a homage to Cézanne at this juncture in Gauguin's career is curious.

104

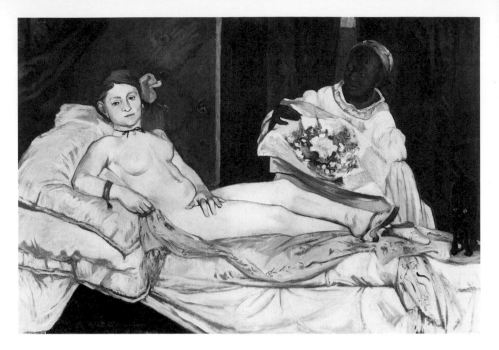

107 *Olympia (copie d'après Manet)* 1891

Perhaps the prospect of his imminent departure from Europe, coupled with his evident disinclination to work on more taxing, imaginative compositions, sent Gauguin back to studying his earliest artistic mentors once more. Returning to Paris for the winter of 1890–91, Gauguin set himself the task of copying Manet's *Olympia* which, in November 1890, had at last taken its place in the Luxembourg. It seems to have been the drawing and the composition that chiefly interested him, for he made little attempt to parallel the extraordinary richness and drama of Manet's blacks and whites, nor was he bothered with the niceties of detail in the setting. According to Jean de Rotonchamp, Gauguin's first biographer, he spent only a week or so working in front of the Manet and completed the copy from a photograph.

107

The exercise seems to have sparked off Gauguin's creative energies once more: in the early months of 1891 he painted a large, gravely symbolic picture of a nude in a Breton landscape, *La Perte de pucelage*. The scale of the work was identical to his copy of *Olympia*, both being

105

108 *La Moisson au bord de la mer* 1890

slightly smaller than Manet's original. He used as his model a young
Parisienne named Juliette Huet, whom he temporarily made his
mistress. As with the Manet, the stark pallor of the woman's body is
contrasted with a darker-toned setting, in this case a reworking of the
view from Le Pouldu over the promontory towards the Ile de Groix,
which Gauguin had already painted in *La Moisson au bord de la mer* in   108
1890. Exceptionally, we have no written account by Gauguin to help
throw light on the obvious symbolic intentions of *La Perte de pucelage*.
The fox, an animal used in *Soyez amoureuses* as 'symbol of perversity',
reappears here, and the girl's defloration is alluded to in the cyclamen
she holds. The painting seems charged with such punning references
and has plausibly been interpreted as a picture aimed at, and possibly
suggested by, the literati in Paris with whom Gauguin was mixing.
Octave Mirbeau was the first owner of the preparatory drawing of   109
the girl's head and fox, presumably a present in gratitude for the
articles he wrote about Gauguin at a crucial moment in February
1891. A few years later, thanks to the good offices of Schuffenecker,

the painting was bought by the rich patron of the Symbolists, Count Antoine de la Rochefoucauld.

The explanation for the absence of discussion of this picture in the Gauguin correspondence is simple. By early 1891 Gauguin had virtually no on left with whom to correspond. Vincent Van Gogh had taken his own life in July 1890. Gauguin received the news without shock or great emotion. Although his letter of condolence to Theo Van Gogh and his failure to attend the funeral have been seen as unfeeling, there is no reason to doubt Gauguin's sincerity when he wrote that Vincent's life had been a painful struggle and he saw this death as a release. However, his motives for opposing Bernard's plan to organize a retrospective Van Gogh exhibition in the autumn of 1890 were undisguisedly selfish, as was his reaction to the news that Theo Van Gogh himself had suffered a complete nervous collapse. Gauguin judged that fate had dealt him, personally, yet another blow. The demise of support from the Goupil gallery came on top of the news that the Charlopin affair had aborted. Now he would have to revise his plans for selling his works and it would fall to him alone to organize the finance for his departure and existence in the tropics.

In a ruthless bid for freedom, Gauguin did not hesitate to abandon those who he felt had failed him. He had progressively alienated Schuffenecker by relentlessly mocking his caution in financial affairs – in short, his reluctance to sink capital in Gauguin's escapade to the tropics – and his acceptance of the yoke of teaching (he was drawing master in a Paris lycée). In January 1891 Gauguin had so abused Schuffenecker's hospitality and friendship that he had finally been shown the door. As for Bernard, already annoyed by Gauguin's disloyalty to their old comrade Vincent, he came to see himself systematically written out of Gauguin's history and plans.

There is no doubt that Gauguin was alert to his potential for publicity. At a time when there was much squabbling in Paris over who deserved the greatest honours for the recent Symbolist revolution in poetry (press banquets were making overnight heroes of formerly obscure poets), Gauguin decided to capitalize on the sympathies and admiration of the young Symbolist writers and 'get himself elected', as Pissarro was scathingly to observe, a 'man of genius'. Pissarro was referring to certain machinations that preceded the sale of Gauguin's pictures at the Hôtel Drouot in February 1891, (a sale which raised 9985 francs), the banquet held in Gauguin's honour at the Café Voltaire on 23 March, and the benefit concert staged at the Vaudeville on 23 May, after Gauguin's departure for Tahiti. These manœuvres included the unashamed traffic in favours, complimentary portraits and begging letters larded with flattery, the courting of influential figures from literature (Mirbeau, Mallarmé 110 and Rachilde), art (Pissarro himself, Monet, Odilon Redon and Eugène Carrière) and public life (Antonin Proust and Renan), and the promotion of Gauguin by turns as a sound investment or a charitable cause. All these moves were familiar and effective short-cuts up the ladder to fame and glory but they nevertheless provoked jealousy, distaste and cynicism in those whose susceptibilities had been trampled underfoot in the process.

Pissarro had assisted in Gauguin's rise in spite of himself, by recommending him to the critic and fellow anarchist Octave Mirbeau. The latter, still relatively green in artistic matters, found highflown words with which to describe Gauguin's art: 'This [man's] work is made up of a disquieting and spicy mélange of barbaric splendour, Catholic liturgy, Hindu reverie, gothic imagery and obscure and subtle symbolism; it combines uncompromising realism

110 *Portrait de Stéphane Mallarmé* 1891

with wild poetic flights of fancy.' Writing in this vein in the Paris daily newspapers *L'Echo de Paris* and *Le Voltaire*, Mirbeau did much to publicize Gauguin's forthcoming sale and boost his reputation. In battening onto the story of Gauguin's 'tormented life' to illustrate the plight of genius in corrupt Western democracy, Mirbeau painted a heart-rending picture but paid scant attention to the details.

Bernard was also caught up in the campaign to promote Gauguin. In a letter to Aurier of mid-1890, he had impressed on him that now would be the opportune moment to bring out his promised article on Gauguin. Sure enough, in March 1891 the article appeared, in the newly launched periodical *Le Mercure de France*, under the portentous title 'Le Symbolisme en peinture – Paul Gauguin'. Bernard was dismayed to find his own contribution to Gauguin's evolution was not once mentioned, despite the fact that Aurier used *La Vision* as the foundation for his elaborate argument. Gauguin was presented as the figurehead of Symbolism, the founder of a new and exciting form of art that could no longer go under the ubiquitous name of Impressionism, an art of Ideas that was essentially, Aurier claimed, Subjective, Synthetic, Symbolist and Decorative.

The claims made for the uniqueness of Gauguin's art and for Gauguin himself as a thinker and visionary were judged by many to be inflated. Pissarro had difficulty in recognizing the man he had known from Aurier's and Mirbeau's descriptions. Fénéon, writing in May in *Le Chat Noir*, spared Gauguin none of his irony, pointing out that such lofty claims led one to expect rather more of his art than it had yet delivered. Gauguin's derivation from the Japanese, from Cézanne, from Van Gogh and from Monet were still all too readily apparent. Gauguin himself seems to have had no qualms about accepting the mantle of genius. He forwarded cuttings of the relevant articles to his wife Mette, whose natural scepticism was quashed by this evidence of the impact her husband had made in Paris. When in triumph he came to take his farewell of her and the children in Copenhagen, she evidently greeted him with more warmth than their sometimes curt exchanges over the previous years had led him to expect. If the success of his sale had boosted his hopes of a more secure financial future, his greatest satisfaction came from being able to impress his wife and family with the news that in Paris his was now a name to conjure with. Promising to return from the colonies a rich man, to make a fresh start and live out his old age surrounded by his loved ones, Gauguin left Mette in early March and set sail for Tahiti on 1 April 1891.

111

111 Paul Gauguin photographed with his children Emile and Aline in 1891 in Copenhagen

112 *E Haere oe i hia? (Where are you going?)* 1892

CHAPTER FIVE

The Search for the Primitive (1891–1893)

When Gauguin embarked from Marseilles he was at last alone. All the younger artists who had been thinking of going with him – Bernard, De Haan and Sérusier – were left behind. The fact was that neither they, nor many of Gauguin's relatives and acquaintances, had been convinced of the soundness of the venture. His wife, indeed, feared that he was courting disaster. Ironically, only Vincent Van Gogh and Bernard had fully seen the point of going so far afield. Vincent had argued that it would be logical for the studio of the south to lead on to the studio of the tropics. Once the studio of the south had opened artists' eyes to the intensity of colour juxtapositions produced by Mediterranean light, they would want to pursue their discoveries further afield. He predicted that colour would play a more important role in modern painting. Gauguin would be the right man to lead such a movement, since he had already proved his capacity to respond to tropical light and colour in the works he had brought back from Martinique. Bernard, for whom travelling with Gauguin was no longer possible, later sought his own artistic fortunes in Egypt.

The search for colour no doubt played a part in Gauguin's thinking, though less of a part than it might have done four years before, when he went to Martinique and was still working in a more or less naturalistic vein. His most recent Breton works, after all, had demonstrated that he could achieve a high intensity of colour with little prompting from nature. A more important consideration was surely that he wanted the stimulus of new, exotic motifs to revive the flagging interests of the 'stupid buying public'. He had fixed on Tahiti relatively late in his planning. When a merchant seaman, he had probably touched in at the port of Papeete, Tahiti's capital, and he clearly cherished the sailor's enchanted view of the islands of the South Seas where life was reputed to be easy, with food and women always available.

As he did not leave on impulse, nor had he thrown over civilized life (despite having made protestations to the Symbolist artist Odilon

113

113 View of Papeete, Tahiti, *c.* 1890

Redon which suggested just such a renunciation), he had taken the trouble to prepare himself with up-to-date information from the colonial office, and immediately before his departure had written to the Minister of Public Instruction, requesting support for his artistic mission. His official letter stated: 'I wish to go to Tahiti in order to carry out a series of paintings there of the country whose character and light I aim to capture.' He was successful in being granted a letter of official sanction, help with his passage out and a loose commitment to the Ministry's acquiring 3000 francs worth of paintings on his return.

Evidently, the officially received version of Gauguin's reasons for leaving France differed substantially from the stories offered in the press by such writers as Mirbeau. Not all critics, however, had been as emotionally swept up by Gauguin's plight as had Mirbeau. The Belgian critic Emile Verhaeren, in the anarchist journal *La Société Nouvelle*, had offered more measured and circumspect observations, usefully placing Gauguin's enterprise within a historical context. 'Another artist who has been drafted into child art is M Gauguin.

Whereas M Minne [a contemporary Belgian Symbolist artist] looks exclusively at the naïve art of his own race and is drawn towards the cradle of the European ideal, M Gauguin expatriates his dream to the Indies and even to yet more remote islands. He is off in search of his aesthetic origins. Also in search of total isolation, exile beyond all art that has hitherto been conceived and practised, complete virginity and, ultimately, of that year in, year out life, far from everyone and everything, which rinses the eyes clean of the impurities of decaying civilizations. . . . Ten years ago, it was argued that the artist should devote himself to the art of his own region, study that alone, imprint himself with his native locality, not look beyond the garden wall. Well, doesn't the example of this painter setting off for the remotest unknown spots point up the vanity of all advice!' So in the opinion of this astute contemporary commentator on art, Gauguin was sticking his neck out by leaving France, but he was not alone in setting himself against the grain of naturalism.

On board ship, Gauguin found himself surrounded by respectably dressed petty bourgeois, all on government missions. In a letter home posted in Sydney, Australia, he stressed his intolerance of such dreary people, and delighted in his physical otherness (he had let his hair grow long) and sense of superiority. These, however, were the very expatriate bureaucrats he came across in his day-to-day life in Tahiti, colonials against whom he set himself with increasing determination and provocation during the course of his exile in Oceania. But was Gauguin as different as he liked to think from his compatriots? His ambition, after all, was to revitalize his mode of production with untapped resources, and as a businessman he sensed that there was a demand in Europe for the kind of images of a forgotten culture he intended to produce – with its mystery, legend, religion and magic – images that could be contrasted with the over-evolved decadence of the West. Circumstances, French foreign policy, the blossoming of Symbolism with its hatred of the everyday and thirst for the unknown and the primitive – all combined to present a promising picture of the possible outcome of his commercial risk.

If Gauguin was convinced that he was the first painter to exploit the Oceanic as opposed to the well-worked Oriental terrain, he was mistaken. A fellow countryman, Charles Giraud, had worked in Tahiti some forty years before, turning out Tahitian scenes for the Salon throughout the 1850s. Artists, indeed, were not new to the

Tahitians, for they had encountered such men as Hodges and Parkinson among the crews of the very first European ships to reach their islands in the late eighteenth century. By Gauguin's day, at least one other artist, an American by the name of La Farge, as well as Charles Spitz, a photographer, were busy recording their impressions of the life of Tahiti, no doubt aware, like Gauguin, and as James Cook himself had been in 1769, that it was a way of life threatened with extinction.

In his first letter home to Sérusier, posted in November 1891, some five months after his arrival, Gauguin reported on his artistic progress to date. He was working hard but as to the quality of the work, he could not yet judge, 'for it's a lot and it's nothing. No finished painting yet – but a load of research which may be fruitful, many documents which will serve me for a long time, I hope, in France.' Later, he admitted that it would only be back in Paris, when he could see his pictures framed, that he would know whether they were good or not. From the detailed chronology of Gauguin's output during his first stay in Tahiti, worked out by the art historian Richard Field, it is clear that he took time to settle down and produce a painting of any size or complexity. He proceeded relatively cautiously at first, as he had done in Brittany, making small-scale figure sketches and studying the tropical terrain and vegetation before attempting to integrate significant figures into this setting. Such paintings as 114 *Montagnes Tahitiennes* might almost have been produced with a view to discharging the promises he had made to the Ministry. But it was ultimately the Tahitians themselves Gauguin had come to paint, and finding models to pose for him in his studio was a delicate business. Gauguin made something of a false start by spending the first three months in Papeete, a much Europeanized shanty town by the 1890s, where his 'official' sanction may have hindered him as much as it opened doors for him; for if it gave him a certain immediate status in colonial circles, it also raised expectations which he was in no position to fulfil. In one of his first letters home to Mette, he boasted that he was being courted by the social élite, the royal family and French government officials, and entertained hopes of making money from portraiture. After a few weeks setting up home in Papeete and finding his way through its relatively rigid social structure (he even donned the appropriate linen suit), he soon showed once again that when it came to producing a fair likeness of a bourgeois sitter he was not the

114 *Montagnes Tahitiennes* 1891

right man for the job. The portrait of *Suzanne Bambridge*, for instance,   115
who was the English wife of a Tahitian chief, was not well liked.

The reality of colonial life in Tahiti was undoubtedly a
disappointment to Gauguin. Although he only occasionally admitted
as much in passing remarks, other witness accounts and
contemporary photographs make clear that this paradise on earth had
been severely altered since the first glowing descriptions brought
back by European visitors. Indeed, in Gauguin's terms, Tahiti must
have appeared almost completely tainted by commerce with
Europeans. Gauguin was looking for a primitive idyll, free from vice
and baseness of all kinds, in contrast to the money-grubbing rancour
he associated with Europe, and some of his first letters home might
lead one to think he had found it. To Mette he wrote enthusiastically,
after just three weeks in Tahiti, about the silence and stillness of the
tropical nights, the gentle, hospitable ways and physical beauty of the
natives. He was waiting, in a new receptive frame of mind, for the

115 *Suzanne Bambridge* 1891

116 *Le Repas* 1891

expected return of creative energy: 'I understand why these people can remain hours and days sitting immobile and gazing sadly at the sky. I apprehend all the things that are going to invade my being and feel most amazingly at peace at this moment.' In the account he later wrote of his Tahitian experience, *Noa Noa*, he elaborated on this feeling of having his over-civilized soul cleansed and rejuvenated in contact with the innocence of the savage, his bad feelings towards his fellow men being replaced by good ones. Such claims have become so vulgarized today by holiday brochures that it is hard to believe Gauguin could make them in all seriousness. Yet, in the same letter to his wife, Gauguin revealed that Tahiti was not all he had hoped for, lamenting that together with Western diseases and culture a large measure of that essentially European vice of hypocrisy had been introduced by Protestant missionaries! This sounds like a deliberate taunt at his Danish wife, for elsewhere he argued that the influence of

the Catholic missions had been equally harmful. In effect, the traditional native beliefs had been destroyed and all but lost from memory in the process of the island's conversion to Christianity.

Bengt Daniellson, an anthropologist who lived for many years in Tahiti and tried the experience of 'going native' for himself, has unveiled much of the reality of Gauguin's existence in the South Seas. After a matter of weeks, living high on the hog in Papeete, those money-grubbing concerns Gauguin had hoped to leave behind him returned with a vengeance. His thoughts were to become ever more desperately fixated on the monthly arrival of the mail-boat, with its possibility of letters and money from France. His own letters home became increasingly querulous in tone as his savings dwindled and the desired funds failed to materialize. He did not hesitate to reproach friends, such as the young poet Charles Morice, whose promises of financial support seemed to have been forgotten. His business concerns were uppermost in these letters, as he chided dealers for their inefficiency, demanded from his wife and from friends that they run errands on his behalf in Paris and give him specific, up-to-date news of his picture sales and critical standing. As had been the case when he first went to Brittany in 1886, the decision he took in September 1891 to leave Papeete for the remoter settlements further round the coast was prompted as much by the necessity of living more cheaply as by any artistic considerations.

Gauguin decided to settle in Mataiea, some forty-five kilometres from Papeete, probably on the advice of a Tahitian chief whom he had befriended. There he rented a native-style oval bamboo hut, roofed with pandanu leaves. Once settled, he was in a position to begin work in earnest and to tackle serious figure studies. It was 117 probably soon after this that he painted *Vahine no te tiare*, his first portrait of a Tahitian model. He later recorded how the girl, having understood what he required of her, disappeared, leaving him in agonies lest she should have taken flight, only to return dressed in her lace-trimmed Sunday best. To a large extent, full-length European-style smocks, like the one she is shown wearing, had replaced the traditional Tahitian *pareos*. The women now spent as much time plaiting straw hats which had to be worn to chapel on Sundays (they had been introduced in 1840 by an opportunistic missionary named Pritchard) as they did weaving garlands of flowers. (Incidentally, 120 Gauguin recorded this typical activity in *Deux femmes sur la plage*.) Gauguin felt he had to work quickly on the portrait lest the model change her mind. If we can believe his account, which certainly has the ring of authenticity, painting these much vaunted Tahitian beauties fully-clothed, let alone naked, was not going to be as easy an undertaking as he had persuaded his painter friends to believe.

By the late summer of 1892 the completed canvas was back in Paris, hanging in the Goupil gallery. (Theo Van Gogh's place had been filled by Maurice Joyant, a poor substitute in Gauguin's view.) From the many subsequent references to this image in his correspondence, it is clear that Gauguin set considerable store by his 'Tahitienne' and, by sending her on ahead to Paris, wanted her to serve as an ambassadress for the further images of Tahitian women he would be bringing back with him on his return. He pressed his male friends for their reactions to the girl, rather than to the picture, anxious to know whether they, like him, would be responsive to the beauty of her face: 'And her

136

117 *Vahine no te tiare (Woman with a flower)* 1891

forehead', he later wrote, 'with the majesty of upsweeping lines, reminded me of that saying of Poe's, "There is no perfect beauty without a certain singularity in the proportions."' No one, it seems, was quite attuned to his emotional perception: while Aurier was enthusiastic, excited by the picture's rarity value, Schuffenecker was somewhat taken aback by the painting's lack of Symbolist character. Indeed, apart from the imaginary floral background which harked back to Gauguin's 1888 *Self-Portrait*, the image is a relatively straightforward one. Recent anthropological work, backed by the use of photography, had scientifically characterized the physical distinctions between the different races, distinctions that in the past had been imperfectly understood. Generally speaking, artists before Gauguin's time had represented Tahitians as idealized types, adjusting their features and proportions to accord with European taste. This meant that hitherto the Tahitian in Western art could scarcely be distinguished from his African or Asian counterpart. Unfortunately, Charles Giraud's paintings have disappeared so we cannot compare them with Gauguin's, but this first image by Gauguin suggests a desire to portray the Tahitian physiognomy naturalistically, without the blinkers of preconceived rules of beauty laid down by a classical

56

118 *Te faaturuma* 1891

119 *Te poipoi (Morning Ablutions)* 1892

120 *Deux femmes sur la plage* 1891

121 *Ta Matete* 1892

culture. Naturalism as an artistic creed, though, was anathema to Gauguin; it made the artist a lackey of science and knowledge rather than a god-like creator. He wanted to go beyond empirical observation of this kind, to find a way of painting Tahiti that would accord with his Symbolist aspirations, that would embody the feelings he had about the place and the poetic image he carried with him of the island's mysterious past.

The preparation for achieving this synthesis was to concentrate once again on drawing, not just drawing from nature but 'searching deep within himself', as he explained to Daniel de Monfreid in a letter of November 1891. An instance of what this approach may have involved is provided by *Deux femmes sur la plage*, one of the few Tahitian paintings to be dated 1891. In searching for an appropriate

120

IA ORANA MARIA

122 *Ia Orana Maria* 1891

pose for the left-hand figure, Gauguin seems to have resurrected and reversed the foreshortened pose of the young Breton shepherdess that he had already used in a variety of guises in earlier works. The generalized landscape setting, which has the effect of pushing the bulky figures up to the surface, has much the same broad sweeping horizontals and arbitrary changes of colour as his recent *La Perte de pucelage*. It is not yet recognizably Tahitian. Gauguin seems to have been intrigued by this combination of two female figures engaged in silent dialogue and not only painted a near replica of the composition to send back to Europe (the first version, exceptionally, found a buyer in Tahiti: a certain Captain Arnaud acquired it for 400 francs), but explored the idea in a number of later canvases, complicating the interrelationship on both the formal and the psychological level.

109

Te faaturuma, which Gauguin translated as *La Boudeuse* (*The Brooding Woman*), must be one of the earliest works from the first Tahitian trip to receive a Tahitian title, although the title was clearly an afterthought, written on the canvas not by Gauguin but by Daniel de Monfreid under Gauguin's instructions. While the gesture of head on hand is the traditional emblem of melancholy and harks back to Dürer, the pose and physiognomy relate closely to the right-hand

117

123 *Une fille* (study for *Parau*) 1892?

124 *Parau na te varua ino* (*Words of the Devil*) 1892

125 Odilon Redon *La Mort, mon ironie dépasse toutes les autres* 1888

figure of *Deux femmes sur la plage*, expressing that typically Tahitian 120 impassivity Gauguin had remarked on to his wife. Here the setting is more specific and contemporary, with its colonial-style room opening onto a verandah, raised above the brilliant green of the landscape beyond. The compact containment of the figure, her asymmetrical positioning and the introduction of strong diagonals, carving up this otherwise flat space, might suggest that Gauguin was once more thinking of Degas or looking to Japanese prints for compositional ideas.

One can suggest such visual parallels with some confidence, given that Gauguin had not left Paris empty-handed: on the contrary, he had armed himself with a collection of visual stimuli, the selection of which must have involved a great deal of heart searching. Several months before leaving France, in fact, he had assured Odilon Redon that he would be taking with him in his baggage a 'whole little world of friends' who would converse with him every day: friends, that is, in the form of photographs, drawings and prints, including the more transportable items in his personal collection, such as Redon's lithograph *La Mort*. The task of identifying the images in this visual 125 library and their influence on Gauguin's Tahitian work has occupied

143

126 *La Montagne sacrée* 1892

several scholars and their researches reveal Gauguin to have remained
far more dependent on Western sources than might at first appear.
122   *Ia Orana Maria* offers one of the clearest instances of the use
Gauguin made of this collection of source material and reveals the
complex fusion of observation and artifice that made up his working
method. This large canvas was the most highly-wrought
composition he produced in his first year in Tahiti, and the first where
he departed entirely from an observable subject to enter the realm of
fantasy. Gauguin considered it a significant and broadly successful
work. In its naïve expression of superstitious faith and its fusion of the
supernatural with the everyday, it is comparable to the religious
works he had painted in Brittany. Indeed, it was still a motif based on
Catholic tradition, for all its exotic, luxuriant setting and Tahitian
figures. Gauguin was not yet in a position to essay a subject from

144

127 Relief from the Temple of Borobudur, Java
128 *Ia Orana Maria* (inscribed 'Au Comte de la Rochefoucauld') *c.* 1891

traditional native religion. The two praying figures, with their hieratic, primitive poses, were direct borrowings from figures on the stone-carved relief of the temple of Borobudur in Java, of which 127 Gauguin owned a photograph, and this long admired example of primitive religious art also provided him with the stylized foliage that forms a decorative band above their heads, masking the more naturalistically treated mountains. The somewhat disparate elements of the painting were collated from a series of drawings and as such the painting perhaps lacks the simplicity and clarity of statement in his earlier religious images. There are signs of indecision on the canvas, such as the late blocking out of the globular-shaped fruit in the foreground still-life, and the awkward insertion of the angelic messenger, whose hovering presence is easily overlooked in the restless floral patterning, particularly when set against the monumental strength of the Virgin and child. In itself, there was nothing particularly novel about Gauguin's iconography. Angelic salutations were standard Catholic themes, cropping up regularly in the work of the more devout of Gauguin's followers, Charles Filiger and Maurice Denis, and in the work of Salon artists. Although the inclusion of the Christ child seated on his mother's shoulder was unorthodox, Luc-Olivier Merson's *Je vous salue, Marie* (*c.* 1885) had 129 used the same device, setting the encounter with Mary in the banal

129 Luc-Olivier Merson
Je vous salue, Marie
c. 1885

130 Jules Bastien-Lepage
Jeanne écoutant les voix
1879

130 context of the French countryside, with peasant and child returning from the fields; while Bastien-Lepage's famous *Jeanne écoutant les voix* (1879–80) had made a somewhat similar appeal to sentiment and attempted the same difficult fusion of an other-worldly presence with an earthly setting. There was some discernment in the judgment of the critic who, when he saw Gauguin's painting hanging in Paris in 1893, condemned it for being 'nothing but a Bastien-Lepage done Tahitian style – all it needed was musical accompaniment by a Tahitian Gounod!' Probably, Gauguin was wise to decide against sending this work on ahead to be exhibited in Copenhagen, when the opportunity arose, perhaps aware that he would need to justify and explain it to the critics in person. It was a work whose complexity was calculated to please the Symbolists but whose conservative iconography could well be expected to lay Gauguin open to further attack from his political opponents.

The meaning of *Ia Orana Maria* is still a puzzle in view of Gauguin's known opposition to the work of the Christian missionaries. Was he

making an ironic comment on the way in which Catholicism had
been altered and mollified in the process of being assimilated into the
lives of the Tahitians, its message understood only in terms of simple,
positive images that were in any case part of their daily experience –
motherhood and childbirth, for instance? If so, his later painting of
1896 *Te tamari no atua*, or *Naissance du Christ*, could be said to make a   131
parallel point. Certainly, the introduction of the Christian concept of
sin, which anthropologists agreed was absent from traditional native
beliefs, particularly sin relating to matters of sexual and material
possession, was widely recognized as one of the most traumatic
aspects of Tahiti's colonization by Europeans, and Gauguin was
surely making an oblique comment on this when he gave his pictures
such titles as *What, are you jealous?* and *When will you marry?*   132, 134

L'*Homme à la hâche* was also painted during this productive period   135
at Mataiea, although according to Gauguin's account in *Noa Noa* it
recorded an incident he had witnessed at Paea. He used a similar
vertical format and tripartite configuration to *Ia Orana Maria*, with a

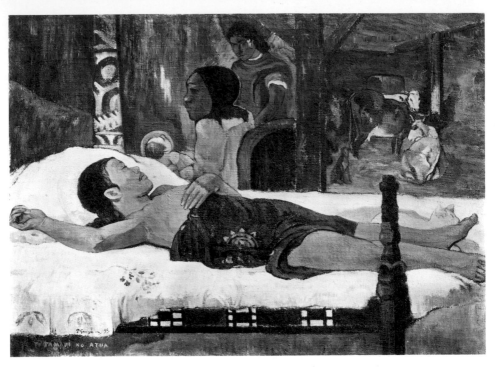

131 *Te tamari no atua (The Birth of Christ)* 1896

combination of a single, simplified monumental figure in the right foreground and a smaller, stooping figure in the middle distance and a glimpse of a more naturalistically treated seascape at the top of the canvas. Here, the simplification of colour into broad areas, broken up by seemingly arbitrary arabesques, which Gauguin likened to the characters of an 'unknown, mysterious language', makes the image a more abstract one. Gauguin used discreet, cloisonnist contours to give elegant strength to his woodcutter, who seems to epitomize the image of the 'noble savage'.

Because this work stands out as such a rare instance of Gauguin's representing an active, working male figure, one is reminded of the fact that it was images of women on which he concentrated throughout his career. Gauguin was, after all, a male artist working for a male consumer market and he was not ashamed to pander openly to that market at times, in spite of his avowed hatred of the base tastes of the decadent European bourgeois. *Vahine no te vi*, for instance, seems calculated to appeal; a straightforward, if somewhat clichéd, image of a Tahitian girl with a mango, Gauguin has given it a

138

149

135 *L'Homme à la hâche* 1891

136 (TOP LEFT) Pierre-Paul Prudhon *Joseph et la femme de Potiphar c.* 1820 (engraving)
137 (ABOVE LEFT) *Joseph et la femme de Potiphar* 1894
138 (RIGHT) *Vahine no te vi (Woman with a mango)* 1892

decidely baroque dynamism in the twist of the girl's body and the
emphatic folds of drapery, at odds with the frozen rigidity of pose he
consciously cultivated in more 'primitive' works, such as the
contemporaneous *Ta Matete*. The explanation for this, as Field has
suggested, again lies in a borrowing. This striking contraposto pose
was used by the Neo-classical artist Prudhon in his *Joseph et la femme de*   136
Potiphar, a drawing of which had belonged to Arosa and a
photograph of which formed part of Gauguin's portable personal
collection. In fact, on his second trip to Tahiti Gauguin made a
painted copy of the Prudhon.   137

In *Ta Matete*, which has loosely been translated as 'We shall not go   121
to market today', Gauguin represented the women who frequented

139 Egyptian fresco from a tomb at Thebes of the XVIIIth dynasty

the public square and market of Papeete, the nearest Tahitian equivalent to the night-life district of Pigalle. It was from the ranks of these women that Gauguin had taken his first Tahitian mistress, a half-caste named Titi, but he quickly found her too demanding and financially draining a companion, unable or unwilling to adapt to the 'life of nature' which he tried to lead in Mataiea. Gauguin's adoption of the artifice of the Egyptian frieze configuration for this painting,

139   closely based on a photograph of a Theban tomb painting in the British Museum he had brought with him, indicates the difficulties he was having in finding any vernacular artistic tradition on which to build. He perhaps intended to pass some sort of comment on these town women, who had become used to luxury from constant intercourse with European settlers. (In this land where sexual favours had been offered freely and fearlessly to the first European visitors, the development of a more Western style of prostitution was an inevitable but tragic aspect of the encroachment of Western civilization, as Gauguin was surely aware.) Alternatively, the deliberate fusion of Egyptian with Oceanic cultures may have been Gauguin's way of acknowledging those contemporary anthropological theories which traced the mysterious ethnic origins of the Polynesians back to the most ancient race of mankind, the red-skinned race whose civilization had reached its peak in ancient Egypt.

140 *Te nave nave fenua (Delicious Land)* 1892

Such theories were cited by Schuré in *Les Grands Initiés*, and we know that Gauguin was interested in the cultural and ethnic origins of the people among whom he had chosen to live. For all its artfully primitive flatness, *Ta Matete* was one of the few pictures in which Gauguin obliquely referred to some of the social realities of Tahitian life. For the most part, he carefully averted his gaze, turned his back on the spectacle of the changes taking place around him and looked to the past for his inspiration.

121, 138 *Ta Matete* and *Vahine no te vi* were painted in the spring of 1892, a period when Gauguin was working steadily and well by his own lights. 'I am in the midst of work', he told Mette in April 1892, 'now that I have got to know the soil and its odour, and the Tahitians, whom I draw in a very enigmatic manner, are very much Maoris for all that and not Orientals from the Batignolles.' (The Batignolles was the area of Paris where artists traditionally went in search of exotic models.) Paradoxically, this productive period followed an ominous setback to his health and a spell in hospital in Papeete. He had suffered some sort of seizure and coughed up blood for several days. Having come through relatively unscathed, his optimism was restored and he was grateful for the chance to continue the work he had begun. By taking each day as it came, conserving his energies and organizing his painting programme so that one day's task followed on logically from that of the previous day, he achieved a steady output of paintings, many of them the stunningly beautiful, major works on which his reputation is founded.

At the end of his first year in Tahiti, Gauguin felt that his achievements were already sufficient to prove to the faint-hearted that it had been no folly to leave Europe. He was merely frustrated, as ever, by the lack of funds for, and uncertainty over the possible date of, his return to France. By the summer of 1892 Mette, for her part, seemed disposed to believe in him at last, now that she could see some hope of reward for the years of deprivation she and her children had endured. Her new confidence resulted from a series of successes. She had managed to sell Gauguin's important early *Etude de nu. Suzanne cousant* for a good price to Philipsen, a Danish artist, and was being courted by him and Johann Rohde, the joint organizers of Copenhagen's Frie Udstilling, the annual Free Exhibition, for some recent pictures by her husband to hang. By chance, she had come across an important article on 'Les Symbolistes' by Albert Aurier,

141 Eugène Carrière *Portrait of Paul Gauguin* 1891

published in the April edition of *La Revue Encyclopédique*, which hailed Gauguin as the incontestable initiator of the new movement. She had been to Paris and met a number of Gauguin's friends and for the first time been recognized and treated as somebody worthy of consideration on the strength of her husband's reputation. Charles Morice was evidently extremely gallant. She also met the artist Eugène Carrière with Morice and reclaimed the portrait of Gauguin 141 he had painted just before the latter's departure for Tahiti. On the same occasion she possibly approached the esteemed republican politican Georges Clémenceau on her husband's behalf to request his official support for Gauguin's free repatriation. Unbeknownst to him, Gauguin had no grounds for continually chiding his wife for her supposed indifference to his fate. When he eventually heard how active she had been on his behalf, he began to speak once more of patching up their twenty-year old marriage and resuming life together in Europe.

This was a hopelessly, even callously, unrealistic promise to hold out given the circumstances in which Gauguin then found himself. But Gauguin had an extravagant capacity for self-delusion, for fixing his sights on illusory goals, as he wrily admitted. He and Mette had been estranged for seven years. At the time of writing to her, he was living with a thirteen-year old Tahitian, Teha'amana, whom he had recently taken as a bride with the full blessing of her two sets of parents, natural and adoptive. Then there was the problem to be faced in Paris of Juliette Huet, who had borne Gauguin a daughter in his absence and who was undoubtedly in need of financial support. Gauguin clearly considered such human casualties as necessary to the cause of his art; in any case, they were common enough baggage for a man of his class to carry around. Fortunately, Mette Gauguin was no romantic, even if she was temporarily lulled into an optimistic frame of mind by her husband's talk; later, she summed up his attitude to life as one of 'ferocious egotism'.

The main reason Gauguin's work had been proceeding so well was that in the course of his research into the Tahiti of the past, he had made a crucial discovery. In March 1892 he had been lent a book by a French colonial, Goupil, a two-volume study of Oceanic life by a Belgian, J. A. Moerenhout. *Voyages aux Iles du Grand Océan*, first published in Paris in 1837, contained a full account of the forgotten religious beliefs and customs of Tahiti, as well as information about its language and literature, political and social affairs. The importance of this document for Gauguin, which ironically he could have studied in Paris, as the romantic poet Lecomte de Lisle had done before him, lay in the fact that it opened the door to the mysterious Tahiti of legend, giving him access to those pagan rituals which he had imagined from afar. He first hinted at this discovery in a letter to Sérusier dated 25 March. He concluded with a postscript, 'What a religion the ancient oceanic religion is! What a marvel! My brain is buzzing with it and all the ideas it suggests to me are really going to scare people off. If people were worried about my old works in a domestic setting, what will they say about the new ones?' It seems probable that Gauguin was in the process of copying sections from Moerenhout's account into his notebook and interspersing them with watercolour sketches. Entitled *Ancient Culte Maorie*, the notebook is now safely lodged in the Louvre. It remained with Gauguin until his death and although probably not intended for publication, it furnished him

142 *Merahi metua no Teha'amana (The Ancestors of Teha'amana)* 1893

143 *Vairaoumati tei oa (Her Name is Vairaoumati)* 1892

144 Letter to Sérusier, 25 March 1892, with sketch of *Vairaoumati*

with the source material for a number of pictures and was used as the basis for *Noa Noa*.

143
144

One of the first paintings to emerge from this period of study, and possibly Gauguin's first attempt at a Tahitian nude, was *Vairaoumati tei oa*, which he roughly sketched in the same letter to Sérusier, describing it as 'truly ugly, truly mad'. According to ancient Tahitian legend, Vairaoumati was the beautiful mortal chosen by the supreme god Oro to be his love and bear his child. She thus became the progenitress of the divine race of the Areoi, a kind of religious order who formed an élite within Tahitian society and lived their lives according to the rules of free love. Gauguin shared the fascination of many Europeans with this concept of unlimited sexual freedom, which had for long been associated with the Tahitians. In the painting, a kind of pagan Annunciation, he represents Vairaoumati naked, seated in the same frozen Egyptian profile that he had used in

121
179

Ta Matete, although the position of her legs and the cloth on which she sits recall Puvis de Chavannes' allegorical figure of *Hope*. Instead of using the horizontal frieze design, he chose a vertical format which involved a steep perspective and overlapping motifs. When he

158

sketched the composition for Sérusier, Gauguin had not yet inserted the rather awkward figure of the divine seducer Oro into the composition, who looks down on Vairaoumati from the top right-hand corner, much as Gauguin's own face looks down on the naked woman in *Soyez amoureuses*. Their union is symbolized by the idol placed on the stone altar in the middle distance.　88

　Just as the nude figure of Vairaoumati was based on artistic sources rather than on a Tahitian model, so too his carved and painted idols were inventions or reconstructions of Gauguin's own. They had to be, since all traces of indigenous Tahitian religious imagery had been lost or destroyed. In *Ancien Culte Maorie*, Gauguin had made a watercolour sketch of the conjoined figures of the Tahitian gods Hina and Tefatou, evidently inspired by the decorative details and stylized figural forms on a Marquesan oar handle. Like so many of his ideas once they had taken visual form, this was re-used time and again. For instance, it reappears in a woodcut, a ceramic vase and a carved statue that, like *Idole à la perle*, probably dates from 1893 (Gauguin　146 mentioned in a letter to De Monfreid of March that year that he was busy carving because he was short of canvas). The imaginary idol also

159

reappears in the background of a number of other paintings, notably
Arearea, Nave nave moe and a landscape which he entitled *Parahi te
marae*, meaning *There lies the temple*. The sacred hill with its
surrounding wall was first schematically sketched in *Ancien Culte
Maorie*, following Moerenhout's description, and then elaborated in
stunning colour, both in watercolour and oil, with the wall now
fancifully interspersed with death heads.

145
126

Perhaps because of the possibility of tying down his borrowings so
precisely in this way (at times they are remarkably direct), Gauguin's
integrity as an original artist has occasionally been called into
question, as though there were something shameful about an artist's
pillaging the past, or such a thing as innovation without tradition,
creativity without source material. Surely the interest for the
historian in identifying Gauguin's borrowings, whether from
Moerenhout or from other art, is not to downgrade his achievements
but rather to understand his artistic practices. His sometimes
repetitive elaboration and recombination of successful pictorial ideas

160

145 *Nave nave moe (Delicious Water)* 1894

146 *Idole à la perle* 1892–3

was not essentially different from the methods used by notable contemporaries working in France, Degas, for instance, or Cézanne. In the absence of original Polynesian artefacts to work from, with the rare exceptions of the Marquesan oars and carvings which Gauguin exploited fully, it was hardly surprising that for knowledge of Tahiti's past he should turn to a reliable published account and make heavy use of the portable collection he had brought with him from Europe. Despite Gauguin's claims, it is in a sense reassuring to discover that the experience of severing himself from his culture did not in fact mean working from a *tabula rasa*; rather, it threw Gauguin more forcibly back on the enduring monuments of that rejected culture. The identification and study of his sources enables us to understand better to what extent the studio of the tropics was necessary to fire Gauguin's imagination and to what extent the appearance of the works he brought back to Paris was predetermined by the cultural baggage he had taken out with him.

147 Gauguin and friends, including Paul Sérusier and Anna la Javanaise, in his studio at 6 rue Vercingétorix, 1894–5

CHAPTER SIX

Confronting the Public (1893–1895)

Late in 1892 Gauguin packed off a consignment of eight pictures to De Monfreid for exhibition in Copenhagen. When describing to his wife the works he had sent, he explained that in order to cater for all tastes (the Danes were presumably likely to be more conservative than the Parisians), he had selected a mixture of relatively 'doux' or mild, accessible paintings – mainly landscapes and genre figures – and some that he considered to be 'raide' or hard, inaccessible. It is interesting that even in Tahiti Gauguin continued to think of his work in these practical commercial terms; indeed, this obvious concern to provide enough variety to suit all corners of the market helps to rationalize what can otherwise seem a somewhat inconsistently diverse œuvre.

To aid Mette in handling the critics' questions, Gauguin provided a gloss on the meaning of the works he acknowledged were more difficult, including the important nude *Manau tupapau* (*The spirit of* 149 *the dead keeps watch*), which he valued highly but which he was certain would be misunderstood, and *Parahi te marae*. He explained, for instance, that the temple in the latter was used for prayers and human sacrifices, relishing, one suspects, the idea of the shudder of horror this would give his European audience. In the case of *Manau tupapau*, he explained that the fear on the girl's face was due to her terror of the Spirit of the Dead. 'I had to explain this fear with as few literary means as possible,' he wrote, 'as was done in the past. So I proceeded thus. General harmony, sombre, sad, fearful, intoning in the eye like a death-knell: violet, dark blue and orangey yellow. I painted the linen a greenish yellow, firstly, because the linen of the native is different from ours (made from the beaten bark of trees); secondly, because it creates, or suggests artificial light (the savage woman never sleeps in the dark) and yet I don't want any lamplight effects (they're common); thirdly, this yellow links the orangey yellow to the blue and completes the musical harmony.'

Manau tupapau is unquestionably one of Gauguin's most beautiful and fully resolved paintings. The flowing lines of the girl's body and the decorative details give it the sensual quality of an Ingres Odalisque, yet the dark, velvety colour range, set off by the jangling yellows of the foreground, and the dramatic tension of the girl's face produce a powerful aura of mystery. Fear of evil spirits and ghosts was common among the Tahitians, the spirit taking the form of the person when alive, hence the strange, brooding figure in the background.

The model Gauguin used was his young bride Teha'amana, a fact he judiciously omitted to mention to Mette. One imagines he had acquired her essentially to further his artistic ambitions and be able to tackle the nude subjects he had planned. He clearly looked on this 'wife' as a dispensable resource, since he planned to leave her behind after a matter of months and move on to the Marquesas islands which, being more remote and more difficult of access than Tahiti, were reputed to be less altered. In retrospect, one might consider that he exploited Teha'amana shamelessly, although such exploitation was widely accepted practice in the colonies. *Manau tupapau* exposed her youthful body in a pose which he admitted would be considered indecent had he painted a European model, and he used Teha'amana's very real fears and superstitions about ghosts in order to give his painting its symbolic, mysterious aura. Two years later, having lost all hope of a reunion with his true wife, he wrote about his experience of this strange, short-lived marriage of unequals. The account he produced in *Noa Noa* was no doubt intended to titillate his male readership: to some extent fictionalized, it was written in a flowery manner reminiscent of Pierre Loti's popular novel about his own Tahitian marriage, *Rarahu (Le Marriage de Loti)*, first published in 1879. It is possible that the description was in the hand of Charles Morice, the Symbolist poet who collaborated on the text of *Noa Noa*. When the first edition in book form was published in 1901, Morice felt under a moral obligation to excuse Gauguin's actions in taking such a young bride, adding that a thirteen-year-old Maori was equivalent in maturity to an eighteen- or twenty-year-old European! Gauguin, who did not hesitate to accuse his fellow colonialists of hypocrisy, was scarcely immune from such a charge himself.

Gauguin needed all his confidence and optimism to see him through the long wait for permission to travel home at French government expense. He had first pleaded penury at the end of eleven months in Tahiti. The bureaucratic delays seemed endless but he was finally granted free repatriation by the Ministry and set sail for France on 14 June 1893. The voyage used up the few remaining savings he had, particularly as he opted to pay extra to travel second class. On arriving some two months later in Marseilles, he was furious to find himself stranded for lack of funds and obliged to await a money order from Paris.

As he had explained to Sérusier from Tahiti, he was impatient to get back to Paris so that he could 'stir things up a bit'. After the enforced idleness of the sea voyage, the autumn of 1893 was an incredibly hectic period in Gauguin's career. Having agreed terms with Durand-Ruel, who thanks to Degas's intervention had for the first time offered to hold a one-man show for Gauguin, not only did he have to stretch and frame the forty-odd canvases he planned to exhibit in a matter of two months, but he needed to ensure full press coverage and court the right sort of audience. To achieve this, having been out of town for over two years, he needed to catch up on all the gossip, find out what had been happening in the art world and see where his reputation now stood.

He sent a series of haranguing letters to his wife, believing her to have failed him in his hour of need at the port-side and demanding news of the exhibition in Copenhagen, which had taken place at the end of March that year. He particularly wanted to hear about the critics' reactions and any sales, since on such information hinged his chances of making this second show in Paris a success. He planned to take the city by storm with the complete novelty of the works he had brought with him. He soon learned that only one Tahitian painting had been sold at the Copenhagen exhibition, a variant of *Femmes de Tahiti*, to Mette's brother-in-law, the newspaper editor and politician Edvard Brandes. (Incidentally, Brandes had already played quite an important financial role for Mette during Gauguin's absence, buying several of the Impressionist pictures that had formerly made up her husband's collection. Gauguin seems to have resented this interference and later tried unsuccessfully to buy back the Cézannes and Pissarros.) As for the critical reactions, Gauguin may have taken heart that not all the Danish reviews had been unfavourable: the diversity of his talents had been signalled by the press. Whether or not Mette reported fully on the reviews is hard to say. Gauguin may well have been anxious about the inevitable comparisons of his works with those of the 'madman' Vincent Van Gogh, since in Copenhagen, for the first but by no means the last time, the two artists' works were shown alongside one another. His worst fears might have been confirmed if word had reached him of the comments made by certain journalists; beside the intensity of life found in Van Gogh's works, his own were variously deemed 'pale and weak' and 'routine stuff'. This was hardly surprising given that only ten of Gauguin's recent Tahitian works had been seen in Copenhagen out of a selection of some fifty works, and a high proportion of them had been early canvases.

Another possible reason for Gauguin's jumpiness at this time may have been the publication, during the period of the Frie Udstillung, of extracts from Van Gogh's letters to Emile Bernard, many of them directly pertinent to himself. These extracts had been appearing in the Danish press as well as in the *Mercure de France*, and although the names of the living artists were obscured, for anyone in the know there was no mistaking Gauguin's identity; the role he had played in Van Gogh's tragic life had no doubt been the topic of much speculative gossip in the Paris cafés during his absence. Emile Bernard, moreover, who had been editing these letters and publishing art criticism in Gauguin's absence, had no desire to spare Gauguin's blushes. Was it perhaps to distance, and by implication to exonerate himself, that Gauguin suddenly decided to draft his own recollections of Van Gogh? His short ironic article, which was published in January 1894 in *Les Essais d'Art Libre*, is notable chiefly for the stress it lays on Van Gogh's 'madness', on his early missionary zeal and acts of Christian charity, on his belief in and apparent ability to work miracles, and his obsession with the colour yellow.

In other respects it must have looked to Gauguin as though circumstances in Paris were favourable to the understanding and appreciation of his new Tahitian works. During his two-year absence Symbolist ideas had gained a wider currency and the standing of his young followers the Nabis had markedly increased. Apart from Paul Sérusier and Maurice Denis, this group included such talented members as Edouard Vuillard, Pierre Bonnard, Paul Ranson and Ker-Xavier Roussel. The Nabis or Symbolists had been exhibiting their flat, decorative and innovatory works regularly in the gallery of Le Barc de Boutteville, the latest dealer to take up the cause of new art, and were being much written about in the Symbolist press. Their names were also associated with the emergence of the first experiments in Symbolist theatre pioneered by their actor friend Aurélien Lugné-Poe. His new Théâtre de l'Œuvre launched its first season of Scandinavian plays in October 1893. The opening of Ibsen's *Un Ennemi du Peuple*, with a programme and décor designed by Vuillard, coincided with the opening of Gauguin's one-man show in November, and the two artistic events were judged to be of equal importance by Charles Morice. Certainly, they were destined to appeal to similar sorts of audience and both playwright and painter, at different levels, could be said to be concerned with the individual's struggle to free himself from stifling bourgeois conventions. However, whereas Ibsen dramatized that struggle within a domestic context, Gauguin's brilliantly coloured primitive idylls set forth the goals to work towards, the rewards of achieving that liberation.

Perhaps of greater relevance to Gauguin and to the way in which his works would be seen and interpreted was the fact that just a year and a half before his show opened, the Durand-Ruel gallery had been the venue for the first Salon of the Rose+Croix group, under the leadership of the self-styled Sâr Péladan, who had recruited adherents from among Gauguin's own former associates, Emile Bernard, for instance, and Charles Filiger. Exclusively concentrating on mystical, religious and allegorical art, the exhibition had proved a fashionable success. However distasteful Gauguin may have found the naturalistic, academic styles of so many of the exhibitors, their success was unmistakably a sign of the times and he must have hoped his own show would awaken the same degree of public interest. He was intrigued and envious to learn that his friend Filiger now enjoyed the patronage of Count Antoine de la Rochefoucauld, the aristocratic Maecenas and amateur painter and poet who had initially sponsored the Rosicrucian movement. Gauguin was not slow to court the Count's sympathies himself, dedicating a drawing of his own most Rosicrucian work *Ia Orana Maria* to de la Rochefoucauld for 128 reproduction in *Le Cœur Illustré*, a new esoteric Symbolist journal the latter was financing.

Roger Marx and Octave Mirbeau were critics from whom Gauguin could reasonably expect continuing support, having been favourably reviewed by them both in the year of his departure. But the untimely death of Albert Aurier in October 1892 had deprived

148 *Pape moe (Mysterious Water)* 1893

149 *Manau tupapau* 1892

150 *Fatata te miti (Near the Sea)* 1892

him of an eloquent champion whose philosophical articles carried considerable weight. It was to Charles Morice that Gauguin entrusted the task of writing an introduction to his exhibition catalogue, perhaps exacting recompense for Morice's failure to send out the money raised by the Théâtre d'Art benefit performance two years before. Whatever irritation Gauguin may have felt while in Tahiti for his young acolyte was rapidly put aside in Paris.

By the time Gauguin's exhibition opened there had already been a flurry of excited press speculation about his return with his Tahitian 'negresses', almost as though the artist were bringing back live specimens from an expedition, as had been done in 1889. Indeed, in the sense that he was still enough of a celebrity for his show immediately to attract considerable attention in the press, Gauguin could congratulate himself that he had timed his return from the South Seas nicely. In their anticipation, such critics aired the clichéd views of what Tahiti meant in the public imagination, views formed by reading travel literature and Pierre Loti.

It is not difficult to imagine the extraordinary effect this roomful of canvases must have had on those first visitors stepping in from the cold, November city streets. The consistency of the brightly coloured, flat and decorative style was more apparent than in any previous Gauguin exhibition, but more noticeable still, in almost every painting the visitor was confronted with Gauguin's ideal, his 'natural', unselfconscious, primitive Eve. Whether her presence

151   denoted an animal litheness as in the stunningly simple *Otahi* (the colour and the disposition of the feet cunningly disguising the debt to

149   Degas), or a dark and brooding mystery as in *Manau tupapau* and *Hina*

153   *Tefatou*, or the sheer physical delight and abandonment of *Fatata te*

150   *miti*, elegant Parisiennes with their consorts were bound to be taken aback by this confident projection of a new rule of beauty.

From the insistent use of an unfamiliar language for his titles and the decision to decorate the catalogue with a particularly barbarous woodcut image, Gauguin sought to underline the distance that now separated him from the essentially urbane cultural expectations and blinkered perspective of his audience. Morice's preface, in all likelihood written under Gauguin's direct supervision, evoked Tahitian legends and presented Gauguin's paintings very much in the

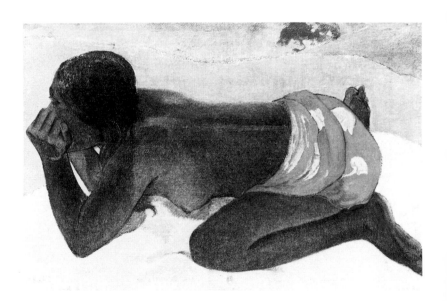

151 *Otahi (Alone)* 1893

terms of Aurier's earlier definition of Symbolism, thereby urging viewers not to expect a documentary or realistic approach to the Tahitian subject-matter. It also gave brief explanations of a few of the more abstruse images in the exhibition, *Hina Tefatou*, for example, and *Manau tupapau*. Somewhat dubiously, it argued that Gauguin had *not* gone to Tahiti in search of novel motifs, but because his spirit had strained under the fetters of European ways of seeing. By staying for a lengthy period and living, so Morice claimed, 'as a native', Gauguin had penetrated deep into the hinterland and essence of Tahiti, indeed, was instinctively in tune with its primitive character by virtue of his own Inca ancestry. Evasive and misleading as much of this introduction now seems, Morice did at least make clear that Gauguin's compositions were an attempt to revive the paradise lost, 'the Tahiti from before our terrible sailors and the perfumed confections of M Pierre Loti', and that he had alternated or even fused with images of Tahiti today images of its former glory – this had been the intention behind *Ia Orana Maria*, for example.

153
149

It is not surprising that, for those who disliked Gauguin's art, Morice's preface could be dismissed also as 'moderniste' and 'décadent'. Seemingly by extension, Morice himself was wrongly described as an 'israelite' in the right-wing journal *La Libre Parole*, an indication of the irrational anti-semitism already rampant in France on the eve of the Dreyfus affair. Many reviewers, however, took their cue to approaching and interpreting Gauguin's work from Morice's words: Octave Mirbeau, in *L'Echo de Paris*, used Gauguin's show as an excuse to heap further abuse on Pierre Loti and to pen another decidedly romanticized portrait of Gauguin's return to savagery, and of his intuitive understanding of the mysteries of Tahiti. As we have seen, Mirbeau was committed to the cause of anarchism and admired Gauguin above all for his rebellious stand against society. Such political affiliations had considerable significance given that in the very month in which most of the reviews of Gauguin's show appeared, the latest in a series of violent anarchist attacks on bourgeois institutions was perpetrated: a bomb was planted in the Chambre des Députés. Félix Fénéon was another critic practically as well as intellectually involved with anarchism, for which he stood trial and faced imprisonment the following year. Although he had virtually abandoned art criticism at this time, he found time to look at Gauguin's show and to give it a mention in *La Revue Anarchiste*: 'At

152 *Mahana no atua (Day of God)* 1894

Durand-Ruel's, the decorative canvases that Paul Gauguin has brought back from Tahiti – barbarous, opulent and taciturn in character'.

Gauguin's attitudes towards anarchism are difficult to pin down. He appears to have shared many of the basic tenets of the anarchist philosophy – belief in the freedom of the individual, opposition to many forms of state authority, the Church, and so on – although he claimed to be uninterested in and ignorant of politics. But Gauguin was nothing if not opportunistic and for the moment it probably suited and amused him to posture as an anarchist hero. The anti-hero was a pose he had cultivated in his self-portraits, after all, and the extravagant attire he sported on his return to 'civilization', to judge 154 from the amusing gouache painted by Manzana Pissarro in memory of Gauguin's one-man show, was calculated to shock and amaze. Yet, in the eyes of committed anarchists like Pissarro and Paul Signac,

153 *Hina Tefatou (The Moon and the Earth)* 1893

154 Georges Manzana Pissarro
Portrait de Gauguin en pied
c. 1906 (Manzana Pissarro drew
this from memory: behind
Gauguin some works done after
the 1893 one-man show can be
identified.)

Gauguin's life-style and now his choice of subject-matter evaded present-day ignominies and represented a 'sell-out' to the bourgeoisie, a pandering to a growing reactionary sentiment. Certainly, Gauguin's work had its admirers among a group of conservative patrons of the arts, such as Denys Cochin and Henri Lerolle, and even the support of Degas and Denis may have rendered him suspect in the eyes of more radical artists.

Political considerations aside, Gauguin was no longer a young man and could not afford to be rebuffed by the critics as he had been at earlier stages in his career. It seems that most critics were disposed to take his pictures seriously in 1893 and 1894. Even if they were irritated by the Tahitian titles and inclined to pass over the relevance of the subject-matter, they paid attention to and some were genuinely intrigued by the formal and colouristic daring of his canvases. Only the most conservative critics were still so disconcerted by the synthetic distortions of Gauguin's style, much as they were by other innovative painters working in this vein in Paris, that they failed to *see* the subjects at all.

Thadée Natanson, in *La Revue Blanche*, was unusual in having the perception to see through the exotic novelty of subject to the numerous references to more traditional Western art, and indeed he criticized Gauguin for relying too heavily on this apparel of novelty to dispense him from attempting any real innovation in style. In substance, these were the grounds on which certain fellow artists continued to carp at Gauguin's success, notably Pissarro, in whose view Gauguin was now 'stealing from the savages of Oceania'. A somewhat more typical review, probably written by Roger Marx, made purely formal, pictorial points, which were reiterated some twenty years later by the influential English critic Roger Fry. Discussing *Manau tupapau* with exceptional frankness, the reviewer argued that title and gloss here were completely unnecessary, 'perhaps indeed we would be hampered by the author's hidden intentions, if we were obliged to pay heed to them. A young Tahitian girl lies stretched out on her stomach on a sort of bed. . . . Is it a polynesian *Olympia* that Gauguin has represented here, or is the chosen subject purely picturesque and pictorial, or again should we suppose it to be a precise symbol? I could not say, but this bronze body, so firm and unified, with its matt flesh, reposing from all activity, is so finely drawn, so broadly painted, so well set off by a décor that is both very brilliant and very simple, that I praise such a work with joy.' 149

That Gauguin was pleased to be spoken of in these formal, painterly terms is indicated by the fact that this was one of numerous cuttings he collected and pasted into a notebook. He dedicated the notebook to his daughter Aline, surely in itself a clear expression of his need for self-justification and acceptance in the eyes of the child he held most dear, yet a poignant gesture given that his daughter did not live long enough to receive it. He would, perhaps, have been happier still with the comprehensive praise of Fabien Viellard, writing appropriately in *L'Art Littéraire*, who admired with equal force Gauguin the painter and Gauguin the thinker. He began by enthusing about Gauguin's successful rendering of the enveloping and brilliant sunlight of the tropics, almost as though Gauguin were still working under the banner of Impressionism, and went on to praise his intellectual understanding of the Tahitian people, which he judged comparable to his empathy with the Bretons. But it was Achille Delaroche, writing in *L'Ermitage*, whose philosophical interpretation most fully satisfied Gauguin and came closest to understanding what *he* felt he had set out to do. Taking his cue from the approach of Albert Aurier, Delaroche set aside all questions as to the real or faked novelty of Gauguin's subject or to the technical and historical origins

155 Page 57 from the Louvre manuscript of *Noa Noa*, with woodcut of Hina and Tefatou from *Te Atua*, photograph of Tahitian girl and a watercolour

156 *Aita Tamari Vahine Judith Te Parari (Anna the Javanese)* 1893–4

of his style, and allowed himself to respond to the works on a more purely subjective level, at the level of their 'suggestive decoration'. He was struck by the way in which 'the serenity of these natives overwhelms the vanity of our insipid elegances, our childish agitations! All the mystery of the infinite moves behind the naïve perversity of these eyes of theirs, opened to the freshness of things. It makes little difference to me whether or not there is in these paintings any exact reproduction of the exotic reality.' For Delaroche, Gauguin's art had the mysterious power to resolve the conflict between the conscious and the unconscious. Here at last, in Gauguin's view, was a critic who had shown himself receptive to the magical inner core of mystery he believed his works possessed.

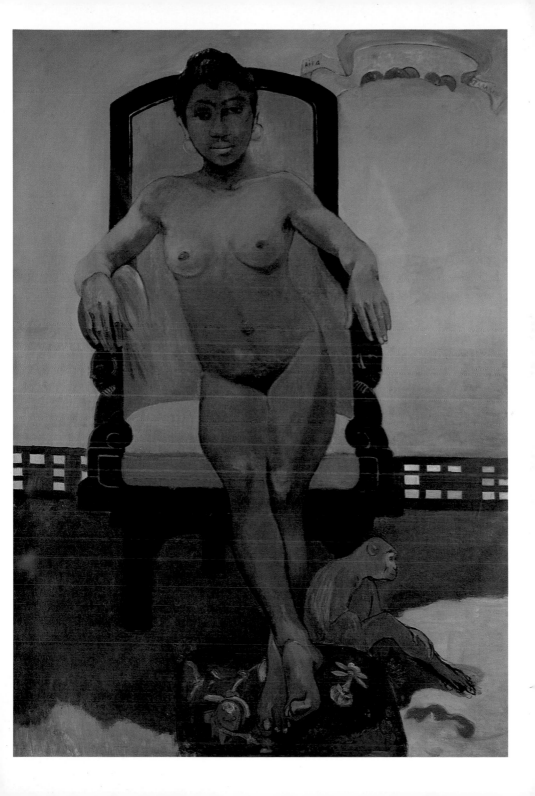

157 *Noa Noa* 1894

158, 159 Pages 67 and 75 from the Louvre manuscript of *Noa Noa*, with woodcuts and watercolours

From a critical point of view, Gauguin counted his one-man show a success and, coupled with the flattering comments of contemporaries such as Degas, Mallarmé and even, grudgingly, Pissarro, it helped to buoy up his confidence. Although certain commentators, including Charles Morice, have claimed that the Gauguin one-man show was a disastrous venture, there seems no justification for writing it off in this way. The disappointment lay solely in the material outcome. Only eleven of the forty-four pictures were sold. Gauguin justified his lack of sales to his wife, blaming the high prices he had been obliged to ask (2000 to 3000 francs each) in keeping with Durand-Ruel's standards. Neither despondent nor complacent, he judged it necessary and opportune to keep up the momentum of publicity, and he set to work to write a series of articles as well as the partly factual, partly fictional account of his Tahitian experiences which he entitled *Noa Noa*, an expression meaning 'very fragrant'. This would serve to extend the public's knowledge and understanding of his Tahitian work. For practical and artistic reasons, as a way of highlighting the dichotomy between the outlook of a Parisian sophisticate and his own one of primitive simplicity, he agreed to collaborate with Charles Morice on the text. (For Gauguin to pose as the possessor of a raw, primitive sensibility was

157

178

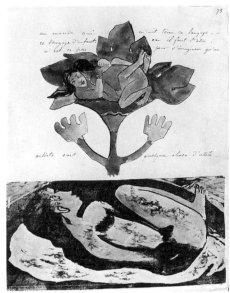

disingenuous, of course, as Nicholas Wadley has pointed out.) With *Noa Noa* in mind, Gauguin produced a series of ten woodcuts, his first experiments in a medium he quickly made very much his own. In subject the prints explored themes already treated in his paintings and represent stages in the cycle of life. The chapters of *Noa Noa* essentially describe Gauguin's feelings and experiences on settling to work as a painter in Tahiti, his limited exchanges with the islanders, followed by his marriage. These personal recollections are interspersed with sections of Tahitian legend, supposedly heard from the mouth of his young bride but in fact copied from *Ancien Culte Maorie* and thus directly from Moerenhout. It is from these legends that the woodcuts derive their themes. Gauguin cut them up and pasted them into the pages of his own copy of the manuscript, often beside watercolours or photographs, thereby creating interesting collages of imagery and meaning.

155, 158, 159

Noa Noa gave a purpose to Gauguin's print-making in 1894, but he cannot have failed to observe the growing importance of print-making in general, particularly colour lithography, within the Parisian avant-garde and no doubt felt an urge to keep up on this front. His competitiveness in technical matters and his readiness to experiment and innovate in different media were constant factors of

160 *D'Où venons-nous? Que sommes-nous? Où allons-nous?* 1897

Gauguin's career. The woodcut was a somewhat neglected technique, despite its long tradition, and Gauguin became one of the pioneers of its revival, with such artists as Auguste Lepère and Félix Vallotton. If the consciously crude primitivism of Gauguin's woodcut style was somewhat out of step in the 1890s, it proved an inspiration in the next decade to the German Expressionists. His woodcuts were in a sense simply reversals of his carved wood panels, worked with an ordinary carpenter's chisel and richly inked, creating sometimes suggestively diffuse, sometimes crisp and bold primitive shapes, touched with colour to increase their decorative appeal.

At about this time Gauguin also produced two more important oil paintings of Tahitian subjects, demonstrating that the imagery was lodged in his memory and could be called up at will. *Mahana no atua*

152

(*Day of God*) was a fantasy of an ancient Tahitian religious ritual, but
the pyramidal design, with the worshippers arranged symmetrically
round the central idol, is oddly reminiscent of Ingres's archly classical
decoration for the Louvre, *The Apotheosis of Homer*. A similar
religious ritual is enacted in the background of *Nave nave moe*, and   145
early in 1894, shortly after its completion, Gauguin exhibited the
canvas next to the works of the Nabis, at one of the group shows
organized by the dealer Le Barc de Boutteville. In both these
paintings and in the bold, full-length portrait of his new model Anna   156
(a half-caste of Indian and Malay origin who passed as Javanese),
Gauguin achieved a new level of decorative abstraction and
colouristic simplicity, setting off his favourite harmony of pinks and
blues with smaller patches of vermilion and chrome yellow.

147   In a rented studio in the rue Vercingétorix, Montparnasse, the winter and spring of 1893 and 1894 was also for Gauguin a time of socializing, living up to his reputation as the celebrated artist from Tahiti. He painted the walls chrome yellow and his own highly coloured works and carvings created a powerfully exotic ambience, as several of his callers remembered. Through his neighbours the Molards, he met a cultured and lively circle of Scandinavians. He also attended openings in Paris – he was seen at the Salon du Champ de Mars for example – and travelled to Brussels to see the first exhibition of the newly formed Salon de la Libre Esthétique (the successor to the Vingt group), which he reviewed. One characteristically provocative gesture made at this time was his offer to donate to the Luxembourg

122   Museum his most prized Tahitian painting, *Ia Orana Maria*, an offer which was unceremoniously turned down, thus confirming and reinforcing Gauguin's hatred of officialdom.

Quite how Gauguin envisaged his long-term future is hard to say. Both he and Mette, in their letters before December 1893, were evidently discussing the possibility of a family reunion, perhaps in a fisherman's cottage on the Norwegian coast. Some time in the opening months of 1894, however, things came to a complete impasse and Mette finally broke off communications. The final straw seems to have been her fury that Gauguin appeared to have no intention of sharing the legacy of 13,000 francs that, fortuitously, had just come his way from his paternal uncle in Orléans.

Certainly, Gauguin's decision to return to Pont-Aven in April 1894 must have been prompted more by nostalgia and a desire to see old friends than by any real intention of producing further Breton paintings. In truth, he had nowhere else to go where he might feel at home. One has the impression that Gauguin relished his notoriety and enjoyed cutting a dash in his strange, exotic attire, with Anna and her monkey in tow. Thanks to the inheritance, he could afford to live more lavishly than before, and there were plenty of young painters, new as well as former recruits to the Pont-Aven school, to whom he could hold court about his experiences in Tahiti. From what we know of his behaviour on this occasion, bragging about sexual exploits, getting involved in a brawl with sailors at Concarneau in which he suffered a broken ankle, and then engaging in legal wrangles with the local authorities, he appears to have accepted that henceforth he would live up to the role of the dissolute in which his wife, among

others, had cast him. He no longer maintained the pretence of being
seen as a respectable family man. The image impressed on the young
British artists he befriended, Robert Bevan and Roderick O'Connor, 161
was one of hard-drinking extravagance and cynical disillusion.

On returning to Paris after a prolonged period of immobility,
during which he had completed very few paintings, he found his
belongings had been ransacked by the faithless Anna (she had left his
work intact, however). Gauguin opened his studio from 2 to 9
December, inviting critics to come and admire his newly completed
sets of woodcuts and monotypes. An account in the *Mercure de France*
by Julien Leclerq made much of the technical strength of Gauguin's
prints and described as 'revolutionary' his new method of making
watercolour monotypes, a technique Gauguin had developed in
Brittany; the monotype itself, that is, single or double impressions
from a heavily inked drawing, was not in fact an untried method,
since for some time Degas had been making such prints, and
frequently working them up with pastel. But as in the case of Degas,
this admirable keenness to try new media was also an indication of
Gauguin's reluctance to undertake new subjects at this stage in his
career; indeed, it showed his satisfaction with the range of motifs he
now had at his fingertips and could work and rework at will.

162 *Faa Iheihe (Tahitian Pastoral)* 1898

163 *Nevermore, O Taiti* 1897

CHAPTER SEVEN

Definitive Exile (1895–1903)

On 18 February 1895, before leaving Europe for good, Gauguin once again put all his current stock of work up for sale. Unhappily, his attempt to repeat his success of four years earlier foundered and most of the items failed to meet the asking price. Degas, who had already bailed Gauguin out on previous occasions, bought several works, including *Vahine no te vi* and the *Olympia* (copy after Manet). This continued expression of faith must have reassured Gauguin that he had not completely missed his direction, even though he was bitterly disappointed by the general outcome.   138, 107

In seeking to publicize his sale, as before Gauguin had enlisted the services of a prominent literary figure, inviting August Strindberg, the Swedish dramatist (whose plays were currently being discovered by Parisian audiences), to write a preface to the sale catalogue. Strindberg wrote back declining the invitation, giving his reasons for feeling unequal to the task and trying to explain what it was he found so disconcerting about Gauguin's barbarous work. This unease of the highly civilized European was, of course, grist to Gauguin's mill and he published the letter as it stood, with his own reply, which sought to answer some of Strindberg's doubts. 'The Eve of your civilized imagination makes you and almost all of us misogynists; the Eve of primitive times who, in my studio, startles you now, may one day smile on you less bitterly. . . . The Eve I have painted – and she alone – can remain naturally naked before us. Yours, in this simple state, could not move without a feeling of shame, and too beautiful, perhaps, would provoke misfortune and suffering.' He extended the argument by drawing a linguistic analogy, comparing the crude, simple language spoken by his Eve with the polished, inflected languages of Europe.

Gauguin was in no mood to heed the advice or warnings of others; he felt he had nothing to gain by staying any longer in Europe, no hope of a reunion with his family, and no will to continue the struggle for existence in a hostile environment, a struggle that was so much

164 *Oviri* 1894–5

more bearable in the gentle climate and friendly atmosphere of Tahiti. In deciding to return there a second time, he was no longer thinking of a future triumphant return to Paris, nor was he thinking of the important work he still had to do. What he had already achieved would suffice to carry his name into posterity – in any case his name had already been raised to the stars. For the time being, his appetite for painting was sated and he told Daniel de Monfreid that henceforth he would concentrate entirely on sculpture, although this resolve did not last. In effect, Gauguin's motives for leaving a second time were essentially negative ones: a renunciation of Europe's decadence, an evasion of personal responsibilities, as well as an inability to back down from the elaborately constructed image of himself as rebel, outsider and primitive, an image which had ensured him a cult following on the streets of Paris or Brittany, but had effectively closed off the possibility of resuming serious, private working habits in France. Not least among the reasons for his deep disillusionment with the Paris art scene was the fact that in the *Mercure de France* of June 1895 his own integrity had been called into question by Emile Bernard in a swingeing attack. An acrimonious exchange of correspondence ensued in which the validity of his reputation was the chief bone of contention. For once, rather than entering the fray, Gauguin allowed others to speak for him and took a gentlemanly way out by quitting the scene.

164

With Gauguin, calculation only went so far and then impulse took over. He had explained to his wife back in 1889, 'You know me, either I calculate, (and I calculate well) or I don't calculate at all, heart in hand, eyes front, I take up the fight bare-breasted.' Had he planned things more judiciously, so his first biographer Jean de Rotonchamp was to claim, Gauguin could have ensured himself a regular income for the remaining years of his life. Ambroise Vollard, who was just on the point of seriously launching himself as dealer for the work of Cézanne and the Nabis, had made a few modest purchases from Gauguin's sale and would have been prepared to support Gauguin with a steady retainer in return for a regular submission of work. Instead, when he left Paris Gauguin had struck up only the slimmest of financial deals with a café proprietor named Lévy, an agreement that was quickly reneged on, to Gauguin's frustration and fury. He tried subsequently to launch a syndicate of fifteen patrons who would each invest in him to the tune of 150 francs a year, but from a distance and with no precedent to point to, this arrangement failed to get off the ground. Back in Tahiti, extravagant spending soon exhausted Gauguin's savings. On arrival in September 1895 he had set about having a spacious, purpose-built dwelling constructed at Punaauia, sparing no expense on the installation of a studio. Already by November 1895, the begging letters to De Monfreid had resumed and Gauguin was once more complaining of his health.

The reason the two-year-old injury to his ankle refused to heal was not just the tropical climate, as Gauguin thought, but the advancement of syphilis, as yet undiagnosed, the disease that eventually led to his death in 1903. In his last years, Gauguin's mobility was severely restricted and he endured considerable pain and stretches of time in hospital; but his enforced confinement to a studio-based practice merely exaggerated an already established working pattern. Earlier ideas were harnessed, developed and recycled as Gauguin's imaginative reconstruction of a Tahitian past turned more and more in on itself. However, the necessary revitalizing periods of contact with nature were lacking in these later years. For intellectual stimulus Gauguin relied heavily on the *Mercure de France*, sent out to him regularly and free of charge from Paris. He had taken shares in the *Mercure* shortly before his final departure in 1895, and there is no doubt that he devoured its contents; it was one of his few means of keeping abreast of happenings in the art scene and in the wider world. But the gap left on the *Mercure* staff by the untimely death of Aurier had been filled by a young and pretentious poet, Camille Mauclair, whose art criticism was decidedly unfriendly towards Gauguin. As a shareholder, Gauguin did not hesitate to voice his grievances about this inconsistency to the *Mercure*'s editor, Alfred Vallette. In truth, by the mid-1890s the *Mercure* occupied a central establishment position and was no longer the foremost mouthpiece for avant-garde ideas. It had been superseded in that role by *La Revue Blanche*, an altogether more eclectic, anarchic review which championed the Nabis and the new star of Paris, Henri de Toulouse-Lautrec. It was in *La Revue Blanche* that Morice published a first edition of *Noa Noa*, without illustrations, in November and December 1897, a move that annoyed Gauguin.

No painting was done during those last few months of 1895, but the wooden cylinder with Christ on the Cross dates from this period. It is a strange combination of the most traditional of Christian

166

165 The new room in the South Wing of the Museum at Auckland, opened in
1892, showing carved panels used in decorating Maori dwellings

symbols with patterns taken from a Marquesan war-club. Its general
shape and elaborate surface decoration probably reflect the fact that
Gauguin had recently seen an excellent collection of Maori artefacts
in the museum in Auckland, New Zealand, where he stopped on his   165
journey out. The museum had on show examples of Maori dwellings,
with their richly carved lintels and structural posts, as well as free-
standing wooden statues of ancestral chiefs, at least one of which turns
up in a later painting of Gauguin's. He made sketches of some of the
abstract geometric motifs, and in adorning his own huts in Tahiti and
later in the Marquesas, he followed some of the decorative precedents
of the Maoris. The *Wooden cylinder* stands half a metre high and was
obviously worked on over a long period. In its use of hybrid religious
motifs, it possibly indicates Gauguin's familiarity with similarly
hybrid symbolic carvings from Brittany, where local craftsmen
had incised their own Christian iconography into druidic menhirs.   167
The carving can also be seen as an attempted synthesis of
Gauguin's 'primitive' artistic sources. Once again, the symbol of
Christ's crucifixion had a probable autobiographical significance;

189

PLEUMEUR-BODOU (Côtes-du-Nord).
Menhir de Pleuven. — ND Phot.

166 Cylinder with Christ on the Cross, 1896
167 Menhir de Pleuven, Pleumeur-Bodou, Côtes du Nord

Christopher Gray has pointed out that the carved hand and foot which appear on one side of the cylinder refer to the present source of Gauguin's physical suffering, his infected ankle.

The increasing complexity of idea and elaboration of surface decoration one finds in Gauguin's woodcuts and carvings also characterize the group of major paintings he produced between 1896 and 1898. One witnesses a certain progression in complexity if one 168 compares the two large nudes of 1896 and 1897, *Te arii vahine* and 163 *Nevermore, O Taiti*, and the two mural-like friezes *D'Où venons-nous?* 160, 162 *Que sommes-nous? Où allons-nous?* and *Faa Iheihe* of 1897 and 1898 respectively. Whereas Gauguin's first single-figure nude, *Manao tupapau*, had been sparked off by an observed moment of terror, these later nudes were more laboriously and artfully conceived. The first borrows a pose from one of the numerous Venuses of the German

190

168 *Te arii vahine (Woman with Mangos)* 1896
169 Lucas Cranach the Elder *Nymphe endormie* 1537

170 *Te Rerioa (The Dream)* 1897

Renaissance artist Lucas Cranach, as well as loosely paying homage once again to Manet's *Olympia*. The idea behind the image seems equally convoluted: Gauguin explained that the reclining nude was a queen, and he had included 'two old men near the big tree, arguing about the tree of knowledge'. This commentary suggests that in painting his primitive nudes, so 'free from shame', Gauguin was nevertheless self-consciously aware of the great tradition of nude painting in the West, and such favourite themes of Renaissance artists as Susannah and the Elders. The motif of the whispering, huddled figures was one of those.Gauguin repeatedly recycled, in works of all media. They reappear in the shadowy middle plane of *D'Où venons nous?*, and the presence of another, somewhat sinister, brooding couple seems to torment the reclining nude in *Nevermore*, whose eyes express unease. More generally, the idea of two figures conjoined in conversation, which was extensively explored during Gauguin's first stay in Tahiti, crops up everywhere in his late work; one of the last, most beautiful mutations is the traced monotype of 1902, where the figures are reduced to heads and no longer appear sinister or conspiratorial, anxious or brooding, but serene and self-contained.

160

163

171

192

171 Two Tahitian Heads *c.* 1902

Gauguin congratulated himself on the rich and sonorous coloration he had achieved in *Te arii vahine*, which he repeated in *D'Où venons-nous?*, the dark blues and greens giving a jewel-like prominence to the clusters of bright reds, oranges and pinks that are so characteristic of Gauguin's Tahitian palette. A more muted, sombre note pervades *Nevermore*, in keeping with its reference to the lugubrious refrain of the raven in Edgar Allen Poe's poem. Gauguin compensates for the elaborate background, where each decorative detail seems charged with significance, by the simple monumentality of the heavy-limbed nude, whose powerful presence owes much to bold modelling. As a painter, Gauguin never altogether renounced three-dimensionality for flatness, despite Cézanne's complaint that he 'only painted Chinese images'. The colour range of *Faa Iheihe* departs still further from reality, with its rich yellows and golds harking back to the gilded backgrounds of early Italian paintings, much as its frieze arrangement echoes Botticelli's *Primavera*, a reproduction of which Gauguin had pinned to the wall of his hut. The progression towards an ever more cluttered surface reaches its extreme here; plants, fruit, foliage and animals seem to serve a purely decorative function.

168

163

162

193

Unquestionably the most important canvas of Gauguin's late
160   career was *D'Où venons-nous? Que sommes-nous? Où allons-nous?*
which he painted at the end of 1897. That year, financial worries and
poor health, as well as the news of his daughter Aline's tragic death,
brought him to the point of despair. He determined to commit
suicide if nature did not do the job for him. Paradoxically, the
personal satisfaction he had gained from his most recent canvases had
rekindled his ambitions as a mural painter, and he determined to
produce one last masterpiece on a huge scale, a work that would serve
as a fitting monument after his death. He ordered a quantity of paints
and brushes from De Monfreid in Paris, and when they finally arrived
he set to work on a canvas almost four metres wide, the largest he had
ever tackled. He worked quickly, so he claimed, by day and night,
using large brushes to cover the surface of the broad sacking, not
bothering with sketches or a cartoon but painting by instinct in a state
of heightened tension. After a month the canvas was completed to his
satisfaction. Gauguin then took himself up into the mountains,
swallowed a large quantity of arsenic and waited to die. The quantity
was perhaps too great because his body rejected it and although he
suffered terrible pains and cramps he escaped death once more.
Returning to his studio, he remained for many days immobile on his
bed, contemplating the great work he had accomplished. It is quite
possible that only at this stage did he paint in the portentous
inscription; Gauguin later explained that it was intended as a
signature, rather than a title, a philosophical reflection prompted by
the picture. By July 1898 when he decided to send it to be exhibited
and sold in France, curiosity about its future fate had helped to dispel
his previous mood of morbid hopelessness.

Gauguin gave numerous lengthy accounts of the production and
172   meaning of this painting, firstly to De Monfreid. Some of the claims
he made about its execution do not stand up to scrutiny, such as his
insistence on having produced the whole thing without forethought
or preparatory sketches. He wished to distance himself from and
avoid comparison with the elaborate preparatory procedures of the
173   academically trained artist. One almost completely resolved,
squared-up sketch survives, done in watercolour and sanguine on
tracing paper. Moreover, several of the figures had their origin in
earlier works. The largest standing central figure, plucking fruit from
a tree, was derived from a small sketchbook copy he had made of a

194

172 First page of a letter to Daniel de Monfreid, February 1898, with sketch of *D'Où venons-nous?*

173 Squared up study of *D'Où venons-nous?* 1889?

174 Pierre Puvis de Chavannes
Inter Artes et Naturam 1890

175 Paul Sérusier *Pont-Aven
Triptych* 1892–3

drawing in the Louvre then thought to be by Rembrandt. The
arrangement of the numerous figures is in a broad frieze, some
standing, some seated. All are self-contained, and apparently
unconnected with one another by any coherent narrative, though
four of them stare out at the spectator interrogatingly. As usual,
Gauguin deliberately took liberties with anatomy and perspective,
especially in the central seated figure seen from behind. His
composition has many similarities, though, with the murals of Pierre
Puvis de Chavannes, whose large painting for the museum at Rouen,
174   *Inter Artes et Naturam*, exhibited at the Salon in 1890, would have been
familiar to him.

   As early as 1891, Aurier had drawn attention to Gauguin's
potential as a mural decorator, calling for someone to offer him the
chance to paint walls. When Gauguin sought such an official
commission in 1894, with Degas's backing, he was rebuffed.
Nevertheless, there was a vogue for decorative mural painting in the
1890s, involving artists as diverse as the Nabis Denis and Vuillard, the

176 Paul Signac *Au Temps d'Harmonie* 1894–5

Neo-Impressionists Cross and Signac and the more conservative Salon painters Henry Lerolle and Albert Besnard. Gauguin cannot have failed to notice the growing importance of decorative schemes at the exhibitions he visited while in Europe, and among his own followers in Brittany; although on a much smaller scale, Sérusier's triptych of 1892–3 has important similarities in subject and coloration 175 to Gauguin's later composition. For all these artists the example of Puvis de Chavannes had been an inspiration, his precedent almost inescapable. Taking their cue from Puvis's work, the themes most artists favoured tended towards the general and allegorical rather than the specific or realistic, in keeping with the anti-naturalistic mood of the times. This did not prevent a traditional, golden-age theme taking on a modern political significance in the hands of an artist like Signac: *Au Temps d'Harmonie* (1894–5) was a projection of an idyllic future 176 when anarchy would reign supreme. In so far as Gauguin looked instead to an imagined past, to a primitive idyll where man and nature had existed in harmony, his painting could be said to express a more

197

conservative, reactionary standpoint. There were numerous possible literary sources for the questions posed by Gauguin's composition. The Scottish philosopher Thomas Carlyle's *Sartor Resartus* had just been serialized in the *Mercure de France* and it gave prominence to very similar metaphysical problems.

Gauguin was extremely anxious that his great work should be presented to the right people under the most favourable circumstances, an organizing task as usual allotted to De Monfreid. Having travelled half way round the world rolled up, the canvas needed some attention before it was stretched and framed, finally going on view at Vollard's gallery from November to December 162 1898, with a dozen or so smaller Tahitian works, among them *Faa* 143 *Iheihe* and *Vairaoumati*. Gauguin suggested the names of various influential people who he felt should be invited to see them, including previously supportive critics such as Roger Marx and Octave Mirbeau. Perhaps in deference to Gauguin's bitter complaints about Camille Mauclair, instead André Fontainas was sent along to review the show for the *Mercure*.

Fontainas devoted considerable space to Gauguin's exhibition. Admitting at the outset that he had formerly felt an antipathy for Gauguin's art, he explained how he had forced himself to make a serious appraisal of these new works. He set aside other people's objections to Gauguin's wilful drawing style, arguing that it was the artist's prerogative to express himself through line as he saw fit. Nor did he think it necessary to carp at Gauguin's choice of an exotic rather than a banal subject-matter; indeed, he congratulated him for having had the courage to leave behind the popular cult of ancient Brittany, whose charm he felt was beginning to pall. In stylistic terms, he was struck above all by Gauguin's emotive use of colour, but criticized him for his over-use of certain stark contrasts (a brilliant red against a vibrant green, for instance). He was captivated by what he took to be the more straightforward evocations of day-to-day Polynesian life, works such as *Faa Iheihe*. However, he remained unimpressed by the large panel *D'Où venons-nous?* with its loftier ambition to address general philosophical questions. Fontainas made the obvious comparison with Puvis de Chavannes (whose recent death had been widely lamented), but all in the latter's favour: 'To represent a philosophic ideal he [Puvis] conceived harmonious groupings whose attitudes were able to impose on us a dream analogous to his own. In the large panel exhibited by M. Gauguin, nothing, not even the two supple and pensive figures who pass through it, so calm and so beautiful, nor the clever evocation of a mysterious idol, would be capable of revealing to us the meaning of the allegory, had he not taken the trouble to write in a corner at the top of the canvas: "Where do we come from? Who are we? Where are we going?"'

A similar verdict was reached by Thadée Natanson, reviewing the exhibition for *La Revue Blanche*. He praised Gauguin highly for his increasingly seductive and gracious decorative forms and for his vibrant colours, but suggested that his attempt to inject his works with literary and symbolic meanings did them a disservice, merely revealing how unhelpful in the long run his earlier flirtation with the Symbolist poets had been. We do not know whether Gauguin saw Natanson's review, but he was sufficiently upset by Fontainas's to feel the need to answer him in a long letter. To the charge that his choice and arrangement of forms failed to communicate his underlying idea, failed to signify, he gave a somewhat evasive response. He argued that mystery, ambiguity, an inability to seize the full meaning of the suggestive décor of Tahiti, were part of his intention. He also justified the occasional monotony of his use of colour by means of an elaborate analogy with polyphonic music. But this questioning of his capacity to convey serious philosophical meaning in a grand-scale work clearly preoccupied Gauguin. When Charles Morice, two years later, tried to raise a subscription to buy the still unsold canvas for the French nation, Gauguin was even then anxious to defend himself against Fontainas's criticism and to arm Morice against possible future objections. He explained that the relation between the arrangement of the figures and the questions posed in the title was in fact very simple. On the left, the old woman facing death, and the idol indicating the beyond, raised the question 'Where are we going?' In the centre the figure plucking fruit raised the question of the meaning of day to day existence, while on the right, the newborn child corresponded to the question 'Where do we come from?' 'Behind a tree are two sinister figures, enveloped in garments of a sombre colour, recording near the tree of knowledge their note of suffering, the suffering that knowledge itself causes in contrast to the simple beings in a virgin nature, the human idea of paradise maybe, who give themselves up to the joy of living.' (One is tempted to identify these

178 *Le Sourire c.* 1899–1900

177 *Nos Coloniaux c.* 1900

sinister figures with Gauguin himself, the wiser but sadder European forced to contemplate from outside the unspoilt primitive life made beautiful by his own creative fantasy.) Finally, not for the first or for the last time, Gauguin produced his ultimate self-justification – the blasphemous excuse that, like Christ, he spoke in parables; just as many of the listeners to Christ's teachings had been incapable of understanding His message, so most of Gauguin's audience would fail to penetrate his veiled meanings: 'Seeing they see not, hearing they hear not.'

In his last years, Gauguin's output of paintings dwindled, especially between 1899 and 1901 when he resorted to taking a desk job for the Office of Public Works and Surveys in Papeete to make ends meet, and also became involved in journalism for local satirical newspapers. He edited his own satirical journal *Le Sourire* and contributed lengthy polemical articles to another, *Les Guêpes*. He entered the fray of colonial politics with no particularly consistent axe to grind and at various times one finds him attacking the Protestant missionaries, pointing out the ineptitudes and corruption of the bureaucracy and legal system (he was incensed at the governor's refusal to investigate fully his own grievances about petty thefts committed by natives), or defending the interests of the French settlers against the increasing economic influence of the Chinese immigrants. He fulminated

177
178

against war-mongering moves on the world stage, commending an example of judicious French diplomatic policy in the Sudan, for instance, because it had averted bloodshed. None of these later writings suggests he held the native Tahitian population in particularly high esteem, or that he had any misgivings about the morality or usefulness of colonialization. Much as a tone of brooding pessimism underlies the superficially paradisical world he conjured up through his art, Gauguin's journalistic writings are pervaded by a world-weary irony which was evidently appreciated by a small, select audience among Tahiti's colonial population.

After 1901 a new arrangement with Vollard ensured Gauguin a steadier income, and at last he was able to move to the Marquesas islands, still further, so he hoped, from civilization. There is a loss of focus and vitality in much of the later painting, due in part, no doubt, to Gauguin's failing eyesight and general health. However, the move to Hiva-Oa produced something of a renewal in his creative energies and in some paintings he equalled the ambition and stylistic force of his previous work. *Contes barbares*, for example, is a major 180 achievement in which the metamorphosed features of Meyer de Haan reappear from the past, a sinister presence overlooking the two figures of Tahitian women, one in the pose of Buddha. Gauguin even embraced some entirely new subjects at this time: *Cavaliers sur la* 181 *plage*, for example, with its undisguised debt to Degas; and he returned to painting landscapes and still-lives, some inspired by the exotic flora and fauna of Polynesia, others, such as *Nature morte avec* 179 *'L'Espérance' de Puvis*, nostalgic evocations of the European culture he had supposedly left behind. Gauguin's last letters to France by no means lack optimism, nor had he lost interest in the progress of his works on the art markets of Europe. Moreover, he continued to experiment at the technical level, concentrating once again on the medium of monotype in which, with no false modesty, he felt himself to have made such revolutionary strides that his achievements would have to be noticed in Europe. The greatest advantage of monotype for Gauguin was that it avoided the need for a printing press. Perhaps in deference to the warnings of Fontainas and Natanson, he henceforth steered clear of deep metaphysical problems in his art, confining them instead to his copious writings. The imagery he explored in such prints as *Femme Tahitienne accroupie vue de dos*, 182 another version of which the sculptor Maillol owned, was simpler,

more archetypal and monumental, based round single figures and
family groups.

One gets the feeling that in his last, lonely years Gauguin resorted
to writing as a substitute for the companionship, conversation and
exchange of ideas he lacked. Much of the autobiographical material
had a propaganda purpose, a setting straight of the record, a getting
back at the critics, a covering over of the tracks. He hoped to see his
various writings collected together and published before his death,
but it was probably just as well for his reputation that no such
publication appeared. His recollections of his contemporaries are not
always fair, affectionate or illuminating, but it is interesting to find his
admission of indebtedness to Pissarro, whose importance, Gauguin
argued, had been unjustly forgotten by so many of his followers.
More often than not, Gauguin's ideas seem to have been sparked off
by an article read in the *Mercure de France*, and the diversity of topics
he touched on, from art and education to religion and politics, as well
as the specific questions he discussed, correspond closely to matters
dealt with in the relevant monthly issue of the journal. His pieces bear
witness to a restless, energetic intellect but they lack organization,
coherence and consistency.

Gauguin died in 1903, in ignominious circumstances. In France
there were even false reports that he had been stricken by leprosy.

180 *Contes barbares* 1902

Having fallen out with the local bishop, he was denied a Christian burial, and because some of his works were deemed indecent they were burned. The inventory of his remaining effects which were sold at auction reveals his colonial life to have been by no means as impoverished or primitive as he liked to maintain.

De Monfreid arranged a small exhibition of Gauguin's work in late 1903 in Paris, but the major retrospective was held in 1906 at the Salon d'Automne. Although Morice feared that the retrospective was held too soon for people to view Gauguin's work objectively, unclouded by the legends and rumours associated with his name, he need not have worried. For a whole new generation of young artists in Paris, such as Henri Matisse, André Derain and Raoul Dufy, this comprehensive survey of Gauguin's achievements could not have

181 *Cavaliers sur la plage* 1902

182 *Femme Tahitienne accroupie vue de dos* 1901–2

been better timed. Their enthusiasm for his bold, unnaturalistic use of colour and decorative simplicity fully justified Gauguin's confident prediction that his work in itself was less important than its consequences would be: the liberation of the next generation from the trammels of naturalism. Gauguin's special contribution to the history of art was inseparable from his biography: the introduction of exotic, 'primitive' elements into the stylistic and iconographic repertoire. This has proved to be an equally enduring aspect of his legacy to the artists of the twentieth century. Did Gauguin but know it, even before his death a copy of the newly published, illustrated edition of *Noa Noa* had come into the hands of a young Spaniard exiled in Paris, Pablo Picasso, and was being carefully and productively annotated.

Conclusion

The extraordinary events of Gauguin's life made him a legend in his own time. Far from seeking oblivion in his island retreat, he lived out his last years as a focus of attention, albeit at a great distance from his native land. Though he died in unenviable circumstances, he congratulated himself on having lived his life in the way he had chosen rather than according to the dictates of society. For this he was condemned by Pissarro and others; in their view, not only had Gauguin evaded his responsibilities, he had failed to produce a social art that could be understood by ordinary people. We have seen that Gauguin by no means escaped the conditioning of the historical times in which he lived; indeed, his decision to exploit the tropics in the way that he did would have been virtually unthinkable at any other point in history. Then again, the problems he set himself as an artist, how to abstract from nature, how to get at the intangible idea through material form, how to convey meanings mysteriously, by means of parables, can only be understood in the light of his involvement with literary Symbolism. Gauguin owed an enormous debt to the support and endeavours of others, and the only reason he could make his claim on posterity with such certainty was because he had undertaken in union with others the enterprise of freeing art from obedience to natural appearances. If at the formal level his example was of crucial importance to the coming generation of Fauves and Expressionists, so too were the examples of Van Gogh, Signac and Cézanne.

It was undoubtedly Gauguin's belief in the ultimate triumph of his supreme acts of individualism that sustained him through the bad times. This belief came about by degrees, by repeated failures to make a success of group ventures. It manifested itself in a suspicion of all joint enterprises, and eventually in scorn and rejection of democratic society as a whole. However much Gauguin tried to play down the literary aspects of his work, it was no coincidence that his appeal was always felt as keenly by writers as by painters. The romance of his life and the way it carried over into his art intrigued and inspired literary men from Huysmans to Mirbeau and to Maugham. Not for nothing did he enact the idle daydream of the Western businessman, an escapist dream that is still potent in the 1980s even though Gauguin's Tahiti, the Tahiti of legend, has been irretrievably sacrificed to the exigencies of a nuclear age.

Select Bibliography
List of Illustrations
Index

Select Bibliography

The Gauguin bibliography is vast and the list that follows is by no means exhaustive. I should like to take the opportunity here of acknowledging my indebtedness to the many scholars of Gauguin whose publications I have been unable to mention. Due to limitations of space, I have listed only those publications I have found immediately useful in preparing this book, in particular those from which I have drawn quotations. An exhaustive and up-to-date bibliography of Gauguin publications will be found in the catalogue of the major Gauguin retrospective exhibition to be held in Washington, Chicago and Paris in 1988–9 (see EXHIBITION CATALOGUES below).

CORRESPONDENCE

Gauguin's complete correspondence is in the process of being edited. For this book I was able to draw on the first published volume, *Correspondance de Paul Gauguin, 1873–1888*, ed. Victor Merlhès, Fondation Singer-Polignac, Paris 1984. This includes all the extant letters Gauguin wrote and most of those he received up to December 1888, as well as other relevant documents such as Huysmans's review of Gauguin at the Impressionist exhibition of 1881, originally published in *L'Art Moderne* in 1883 (see Chapter 1). All references in the text to letters of this period are taken from this volume and translated by the author. For later correspondence the main sources are still: P. *Gauguin: Letters to his Wife and Friends*, ed. M. Malingue, trans. H. Stenning, London n.d. (1948); P. Gauguin, *Lettres de Gauguin à Georges Daniel de Monfreid*, ed. V. Ségalen, Paris 1930 (updated edition 1950); *Paul Gauguin: 45 Lettres à Vincent, Theo et Jo Van Gogh*, ed. D. Cooper, Rijksmuseum Vincent Van Gogh, Lausanne 1983.

OTHER WRITINGS BY GAUGUIN

There is no complete edition of Gauguin's writings. Extracts from his writings are to be found in Gauguin, *Oviri, écrits d'un sauvage*, ed. D. Guérin, Paris 1974. References in the text to Gauguin's writings, both to his published articles and to the unpublished *Notes Synthétiques* of 1884–5 and *Avant et Après* of 1903, are taken from this source. A translation of *Avant et Après* by Van Wyck Brooks appeared as *Paul Gauguin's Intimate Journals* in 1923 (new edition New York and London 1949). The facsimile edition of Gauguin's *Cahier pour Aline* of 1893, Fondation Jacques Doucet, Société des Amis de la Bibliothèque d'Art et Archéologie de l'Université de Paris 1963, contains the cuttings from most of the critical reviews of Gauguin's one-man show of 1893 (see chapter 6). The most useful recent account of *Noa Noa*, its genesis, meaning and transformation through successive editions, is *Noa Noa: Gauguin's Tahiti*, edited and with text by N. Wadley, Oxford 1985. For Gauguin's later journalism see B. Danielsson and P. O'Reilly, *Gauguin: Journaliste à Tahiti et ses articles des 'Guêpes'*, Paris 1966.

OTHER DOCUMENTARY SOURCES

On Gauguin's youth and family origins see U. Marks-Vandenbroucke, *Gazette des Beaux-Arts*, nos 1044–47, 1958. *Correspondance de Camille Pissarro, 1865–1885*, vol. 1, ed. Janine Bailly-Herzberg, Paris 1980. Camille Pissarro, *Lettres à son fils Lucien*, ed. John Rewald, Paris 1950. Félix Fénéon, *Œuvres plus que complètes*, 2 vols, Paris and Geneva 1970. Octave Mirbeau, *Des Artistes*, Paris 1986.

MONOGRAPH STUDIES

B. Danielsson, *Gauguin in the South Seas*, London 1965. F. Cachin, *Gauguin*, Paris 1968. M. Roskill, *Van Gogh, Gauguin and the Impressionist Circle*, London 1970. A. Bowness, *Gauguin*, London 1971. W. Anderson, *Gauguin's Paradise Lost*, London 1972. R. Field, *Paul Gauguin: The Paintings of the First Voyage to Tahiti*, New York 1977. F. Orton and G. Pollock, 'Les Données Bretonnantes: la Prairie de Représentation', *Art History*, September 1980, reprinted in *Modern Art and Modernism: A Critical Anthology*, ed. F. Frascina and C. Harrison, London 1982. B. Thomson, *Gauguin and 'Post-Impressionism'*, Block 111, Arts: A Third-Level Course, Modern Art and Modernism, The Open University 1983. J. Teilhet-Fisk, *Paradise Reviewed: An Interpretation of Gauguin's Polynesian Symbolism*, Michigan 1983. A useful introduction to the Europeanization of Tahiti is D. Howarth *Tahiti: A Paradise Lost*, London 1983.

ŒUVRE CATALOGUES

In anticipation of the revised *catalogue raisonné* which was in preparation by the late Douglas Cooper and due to be published by the Fondation Wildenstein, the most complete guide to Gauguin's paintings remains G. Wildenstein and R. Cogniat, *Paul Gauguin: 1, Catalogue*, Paris 1964, although it has many flaws. The succinct Rizzoli publication, re-edited by Flammarion as *Tout l'Œuvre Peint de Gauguin*, Paris 1981, is a useful alternative, despite its postage-stamp size reproductions. For Gauguin's works in other media see M. Bodelsen, *Gauguin's Ceramics*, London 1964; C. Gray, *Sculpture and Ceramics of Paul Gauguin*, Baltimore 1963; M. Guérin, *L'Œuvre gravé de Gauguin*, 2 vols, Paris 1927.

EXHIBITION CATALOGUES

Gauguin and the Pont-Aven School, Tate Gallery, London 1966. R. Field, *Paul Gauguin Monotypes*, Philadelphia Museum of Art, Philadelphia 1973. M. Bodelsen, *Gauguin and Van Gogh in Copenhagen in 1893*, Ordrupgaard, Copenhagen 1984. K. Varnedoe, 'Gauguin', *Primitivism in Modern Art*, Museum of Modern Art, New York 1984. *Le Chemin de Gauguin: genèse et rayonnement*, Musée du Prieuré, Saint Germain-en-Laye 1985. Forthcoming: *Gauguin*, National Gallery of Art, Washington; Art Institute of Chicago; Musée d'Orsay, Paris 1988 (dates to be confirmed).

List of Illustrations

All works are by Paul Gauguin unless otherwise stated. Measurements are given in centimetres and inches, height before width

1 *Autoportrait au chapeau* (*Self-Portrait wearing a Hat*) 1893. Oil on canvas 46 × 38 (18⅛ × 15). Musée d'Orsay, Paris. Photo Réunion des musées nationaux

2 *Gauguin devant son chevalet* (*Gauguin at his Easel*) 1885. Oil on canvas 65 × 54 (25⅝ × 21¼). Private Collection, Switzerland

3 *Pastorales Tahitiennes* (*Tahitian Pastoral*) 1892. Oil on canvas 86 × 113 (33⅞ × 44½). Hermitage Museum, Leningrad

4 *Mette Gauguin en robe de soir* (*Mette Gauguin in Evening Dress*) 1884. Oil on canvas 65 × 54 (25⅝ × 21¼). National Gallery, Oslo

5 *La Mère de l'artiste* (*The Mother of the Artist*) 1889. Oil on canvas 41 × 33 (16⅛ × 13). Staatsgalerie, Stuttgart

6 *Paysage avec peupliers* (*Landscape with Poplars*) 1875. Oil on canvas 81 × 101 (31⅞ × 39¾). Indianapolis Museum of Art, Estate of Kurt F. Pantzer

7 *Paysage c.* 1873. Oil on canvas 50.5 × 81.6 (19⅞ × 32⅛). Fitzwilliam Museum, Cambridge

8 Camille Pissarro *The Côte des Bœufs at L'Hermitage, near Pontoise* 1877. Oil on canvas 115 × 87.5 (44¼ × 34½). National Gallery, London

9 *Les Pommiers en fleurs* (*Apple Trees in Blossom*) 1879. Oil on canvas 88 × 115 (34⅝ × 45¼). Private Collection

10 *Le Jardin, rue Carcel* (*Garden in the rue Carcel*) 1881. Oil on canvas 87 × 114 (34¼ × 44⅞). Ny Carlsberg Glyptotek, Copenhagen

11 Georges Manzana Pissarro *An Impressionist Picnic c. 1881* (No date). Pen and ink. Private Collection, Philadelphia

12 Paul Cézanne *Montagnes, l'Estaque* (*Mountains at l'Estaque*) *c.* 1878–80. Oil on canvas 53.3 × 72.4 (21 × 28½). National Museum of Wales, Cardiff

13 *Paysage provençal d'après Cézanne* (*Provençal Landscape after Cézanne*) 1885. Fan, gouache 28 × 55 (11 × 21⅝). Ny Carlsberg Glyptotek, Copenhagen

14 Camille Pissarro *Paul Gauguin sculptant la Dame en promenade* (*Paul Gauguin sculpting Woman Walking*) *c.* 1881. Black chalk 29.5 × 23.3 (11⅝ × 9⅛). National Museum, Stockholm

15 Portrait bust of Mette Gauguin, 1879. White marble h. 34 (13¼). Courtauld Institute Galleries, London

16 Bust of Clovis Gauguin, 1881. Head of wax, painted, torso of carved walnut h. 40 (15¾). Private Collection

17 *La Petite rêve, étude* (*Little Girl Dreaming, study*) 1881. Oil on canvas 59.5 × 73.5 (23⅜ × 28⅞). The Ordrupgaard Collection, Copenhagen

18 *Intérieur du peintre à Paris, rue Carcel* (*Interior of the Painter's House, rue Carcel*) 1881. Oil on canvas 130 × 162 (51⅛ × 63¾). National Gallery, Oslo

19 *Nature morte au profil de Laval* (*Still-Life with Profile of Laval*) 1886. Oil on canvas 46 × 38 (18⅛ × 15). The Josefowitz Collection

20 *Nature morte dans un intérieur* (*Still-Life in an Interior*) 1885. Oil on canvas 60 × 74 (23⅝ × 29). Private Collection, Switzerland

21 *Etude de nu. Suzanne cousant* (*Study of a Nude. Suzanne Sewing*) 1880. Oil on canvas 115 × 80 (45¼ × 31½). Ny Carlsberg Glyptotek, Copenhagen

22 *Le Port de Rouen* (*The Port of Rouen*) 1884. Oil on canvas 47 × 65 (18⅛ × 25⅝). Collection: The Reader's Digest Association, Inc.

23 *Les Maraîchers de Vaugirard* (*The Market Gardens at Vaugirard*) *c.* 1879. Oil on canvas 64 × 100 (26 × 39½). Smith College Museum of Art, Northampton, Massachusetts

24 *Végétation tropicale, Martinique* (*Tropical Vegetation, Martinique*) 1887. Oil on canvas 116 × 89 (45⅝ × 35). National Galleries of Scotland, Edinburgh

25 *Vaches au repos* (*Landscape with Cows*) 1885. Oil on canvas 64 × 80 (25¼ × 31½). Museum Boymans-van Beuningen, Rotterdam

26 Breton Girl (Study for *Les Quatre Bretonnes*), 1886. Coloured chalk 48 × 32 (18⅞ × 12⅝). The Burrell Collection, Glasgow Museums and Art Galleries

27 Vase with Breton Girls, 1886–7. Glazed stoneware h. 29.5 (11½). Musées Royaux d'Art et d'Histoire, Brussels

28 Georges Seurat *Un Dimanche d'Eté à l'Ile de la Grande Jatte* (*Summer Sunday on the Island of La Grande Jatte*) 1884–6. Oil on canvas 207.6 × 308 (81¾ × 121¼). Courtesy of the Art Institute of Chicago, Helen Birch Bartlett Memorial Collection

29 *Baigneuses à Dieppe* (*Bathers at Dieppe*) 1885. Oil on canvas 38.1 × 46.2 (15 × 18¼). National Museum of Western Art, Tokyo

30 Vase in the manner of Kate Greenaway, made in the studio of Ernest Chaplet for the Haviland firm, *c.* 1884. Albis Collection, France

31 *Les Quatre Bretonnes* (*The Four Breton Girls*) 1886. Oil on canvas 72 × 90 (28⅜ × 35½). Neue Pinakothek, Munich

32 Pascal Dagnan-Bouveret *Breton Women at a Pardon* 1887. Oil on canvas 125 × 141 (49¼ × 55½). Calouste Gulbenkian Museum, Lisbon

33 Edgar Degas *Femme nue debout* (*Standing Nude*) *c.* 1880–3. Pastel and black chalk on paper 48.2 × 61 (19 × 24).

Musée d'Orsay, Paris. Photo Réunion des musées nationaux
34 Study for *Deux baigneuses* (*Two Bathers*) 1886–7. Black chalk and pastel on paper 58.4 × 34.9 (23 × $13\frac{3}{4}$). Courtesy of the Art Institute of Chicago, Gift of Gilbert W. Chapman in Memory of Charles B. Goodspeed
35 *Deux baigneuses* (*Two Bathers*) 1887. Oil on canvas 87 × 69 ($36\frac{1}{4}$ × 28). Museo Nacional de Bellas Artes, Buenos Aires
36 *La Bergère Bretonne* (*Breton Shepherdess*) 1886. Oil on canvas 60 × 68 ($23\frac{5}{8}$ × $26\frac{3}{4}$). From the collection at the Laing Art Gallery, Newcastle upon Tyne. Reproduced by permission of Tyne and Wear Museums Service
37 *Jeunes Bretons au bain* (*Young Breton Boys Bathing*) 1886. Oil on canvas 60 × 74 ($23\frac{5}{8}$ × 29). Private Collection
38 Cup decorated with the figure of a bathing girl, 1888. Stoneware h. 29 ($11\frac{3}{8}$). Private Collection
39 Vase decorated with the half-length figure of a woman, exhibited 1893. Stoneware h. 21.6 ($8\frac{1}{2}$). Kunstindustrimuseum, Copenhagen
40 Rectangular Jardinière, 1887. Stoneware and barbotine 27 × 40 × 22 ($10\frac{5}{8}$ × $15\frac{3}{4}$ × $8\frac{1}{2}$). Private Collection
41 *Bord de mer, Martinique* (*By the Sea, Martinique*) 1887. Oil on canvas 54 × 90 ($21\frac{1}{4}$ × $35\frac{1}{2}$). Ny Carlsberg Glyptotek, Copenhagen
42 *Allées et venues, Martinique* (*Comings and Goings, Martinique*) 1887. Oil on canvas 72 × 92 ($28\frac{3}{8}$ × $36\frac{1}{4}$). Thyssen-Bornemisza Collection, Lugano
43 Two Women from Martinique, 1887. Charcoal and pastel on paper 48.5 × 64 ($19\frac{1}{8}$ × $25\frac{1}{8}$). Musée des Arts Africains et Océaniens, Paris. Photo Réunion des musées nationaux
44 *Les Mangos, Martinique* (*Mango Pickers, Martinique*) 1887. Oil on canvas 89 × 116 (35 × $45\frac{1}{2}$). Collection National Museum Vincent Van Gogh, Amsterdam
45 *Hiver, ou petit Breton arrangeant son sabot* (*Winter or Young Breton Boy Adjusting his Clog*) 1888. Oil on canvas 90 × 71 ($35\frac{1}{2}$ × 28). Ny Carlsberg Glyptotek, Copenhagen
46 *La Ronde des petites Bretonnes* (*Breton Girls Dancing, Pont-Aven*) 1888. Oil on canvas 70.5 × 87.2 ($27\frac{3}{4}$ × $34\frac{3}{8}$). National Gallery of Art, Washington, Collection of Mr and Mrs Paul Mellon
47 *Lutte Bretonne* (*Children Wrestling*) 1888. Oil on canvas 93 × 73 ($36\frac{1}{4}$ × $28\frac{3}{4}$). The Josefowitz Collection
48 *Les Premières fleurs, les Bretonnes aux Avins* (*First Flowers, Breton Women at Les Avins*) 1888. Oil on canvas 70 × 92 ($27\frac{1}{2}$ × $36\frac{1}{4}$). Private Collection. Photo courtesy Sotheby's, London
49 Edgar Degas *Danseuse ajustant son soulier* (*Dancer adjusting her slipper*) *c.* 1880. Pastel on paper 48.2 × 61 (19 × 24). The Dixon Gallery and Gardens, Memphis, Tennessee, Bequest of Mr and Mrs Hugo Dixon
50 Page of sketches after Degas, *c.* 1888–9. Black chalk 34 × 22.5 ($13\frac{3}{8}$ × $8\frac{7}{8}$). Musée du Louvre, Paris, Cabinet des Dessins. Photo Réunion des musées nationaux
51 Louis Anquetin *Avenue de Clichy, cinq heures du soir* (*Avenue de Clichy, Five O'Clock in the Evening*) 1887. Oil on canvas 69 × 53 ($27\frac{1}{8}$ × $20\frac{7}{8}$). Courtesy Wadsworth Atheneum, Hartford. Ella Gallup Sumner and Mary Catlin Sumner Collection
52 Emile Bernard *Les Bretonnes dans la prairie* (*Breton Women in the Meadow*) 1888. Oil on canvas 74 × 92 (29 × $36\frac{1}{4}$). Private Collection. Photo Giraudon
53 *La Vision après le Sermon. La Lutte de Jacob avec l'Ange* (*Vision after the Sermon. Jacob wrestling with the Angel*) 1888. Oil on canvas 73 × 92 ($28\frac{3}{4}$ × $36\frac{1}{4}$). National Galleries of Scotland, Edinburgh
54 *Madeleine Bernard* 1888. Oil on canvas 72 × 58 ($28\frac{3}{8}$ × $22\frac{7}{8}$) Musée de Peinture et de Sculpture, Grenoble
55 *Vendanges à Arles. Misères humaines* (*Grape Harvest at Arles. Human Anguish*) 1888. Oil on canvas 73 × 92 ($28\frac{3}{4}$ × $36\frac{1}{4}$). The Ordrupgaard Collection, Copenhagen
56 *Autoportrait. Les Misérables* (*Self-Portrait*) 1888. Oil on canvas 45 × 55 ($17\frac{3}{4}$ × $21\frac{5}{8}$). Collection National Museum Vincent Van Gogh, Amsterdam
57 *Van Gogh peignant des soleils* (*Van Gogh painting Sunflowers*) 1888. Oil on canvas 73 × 92 ($28\frac{3}{4}$ × $36\frac{1}{4}$). Collection National Museum Vincent Van Gogh, Amsterdam
58 *L'Arlésienne. Mme Ginoux* (*The Woman from Arles*) 1888. Charcoal 56 × 48.4 (22 × 19). Private Collection
59 *Café de nuit à Arles* (*Night Café at Arles*) 1888. Oil on canvas 73 × 92 ($28\frac{3}{4}$ × $36\frac{1}{4}$). Pushkin Museum, Moscow
60 Vincent Van Gogh *The Night Café* 1888. Oil on canvas 72.4 × 92.1 ($28\frac{1}{2}$ × $36\frac{1}{4}$). Yale University Art Gallery, bequest of Stephen Carlton Clark, B.A. 1903
61 *Arlésiennes* (*Women from Arles*) 1888. Black chalk. Page 51 from Arles Sketchbook. The Israel Museum, Jerusalem, Gift of Mr Sam Saltz, NYC. America-Israel Cultural Foundation
62 *Arlésiennes au jardin public, mistral* (*Women from Arles in the Public Garden, the Mistral*) 1888. Oil on canvas 73 × 91.5 ($28\frac{3}{4}$ × 36). Courtesy of the Art Institute of Chicago, Mr and Mrs Lewis L. Coburn Memorial Collection
63 Vincent Van Gogh *Memory of the Garden at Etten* 1888. Oil on canvas 73.5 × 92.5 (29 × $36\frac{3}{8}$). Hermitage Museum, Leningrad
64 *Ondine* 1889. Oil on canvas 92 × 72 ($36\frac{1}{4}$ × $28\frac{1}{4}$). The Cleveland Museum of Art, Gift of Mr and Mrs William Powell Jones
65 *Dans les foins. En pleine chaleur* (*In the Hay. In the Heat of the Day*) 1888. Oil on canvas 73 × 92 ($28\frac{3}{4}$ × $36\frac{1}{4}$). Private Collection
66 Eugène Delacroix *The Death of Sardanapalus* (detail) 1827. Oil on canvas 395 × 495 ($155\frac{1}{2}$ × 195). Musée du Louvre, Paris. Photo Bulloz
67 *Autoportrait* (*Self-Portrait*) 1888. Oil on canvas 46 × 38 ($18\frac{1}{8}$ × 15). Pushkin Museum, Moscow
68 *Nature morte à l'estampe japonaise* (*Still-Life with Japanese Print*) 1889. Oil on canvas 73 × 92 ($28\frac{3}{4}$ × $36\frac{1}{4}$). Museum of Modern Art, Teheran
69 Peruvian mummy from the northern Andes, 1100–1400. Musée de l'Homme, Paris
70 *Eve. Pas écouter li li menteur* (*Eve. Don't Listen to the Liar*) 1889. Watercolour and pastel on paper 33.7 × 31.1 ($13\frac{1}{4}$ × $12\frac{1}{4}$). Courtesy of the Marion Koogler McNay Art Museum, San Antonio, Texas, Bequest of Marion Koogler McNay
71 *Femmes se baignant. La vie et la mort* (*Women Bathing. Life*

and Death) 1889. Oil on canvas 92 × 73 ($36\frac{1}{4}$ × $28\frac{3}{4}$). Mohammad Mahmoud Khalil Museum, Cairo

72 *La Belle Angèle. Portrait de Mme Satre* (*Portrait of Mme Satre*) 1889. Oil on canvas 92 × 72 ($36\frac{1}{4}$ × $28\frac{1}{4}$). Musée d'Orsay, Paris. Photo Réunion des musées nationaux

73 *La Famille Schuffenecker* (*The Schuffenecker Family*) 1889. Oil on canvas 73 × 92 ($28\frac{3}{4}$ × $36\frac{1}{4}$). Musée d'Orsay, Paris. Photo Réunion des musées nationaux

74 *Autoportrait au Christ jaune* (*Self-Portrait with Yellow Christ*) 1889. Oil on canvas 38 × 46 (15 × $18\frac{1}{8}$). Private Collection. Photo Giraudon

75 *Bretonnes à la barrière* (*Breton Women at the Gate*) 1889. Zincograph on yellow paper 17 × 21.4 ($6\frac{5}{8}$ × $8\frac{1}{2}$). Courtesy of the Art Institute of Chicago, McKee Memorial Collection

76 *Les Cigales et les fourmis* (*The Grasshoppers and the Ants*) 1889. Zincograph on yellow paper 20.3 × 26 (8 × $10\frac{1}{4}$). National Gallery of Art, Washington. Lessing Rosenwald Collection

77 *Aux Roches noires*, frontispiece of the Volpini exhibition catalogue, 1889

78 Paul Sérusier *Le Talisman, le bois d'amour* (*The Talisman, Landscape in the Bois d'Amour*) 1888. Oil on wood 27 × 22 ($10\frac{3}{4}$ × $8\frac{3}{4}$). Musée d'Orsay, Paris. Photo Réunion des musées nationaux

79 The Palais des Colonies at the Universal Exhibition 1889, Paris. From E. Monod, *Livre d'Or de l'Exposition Universelle, Album* 1890

80 Page of studies of figures in costume at the Universal Exhibition (Annamites and Arabs), 1889? Black chalk 30.5 × 23.5 (12 × $9\frac{1}{4}$). Musée du Louvre, Paris, Cabinet des Dessins. Photo Réunion des musées nationaux

81 *La Femme noire* (*The Black Woman*) 1889. Stoneware h. 50 ($19\frac{3}{4}$). Nassau County Museum, Sands Point, New York

82 *Eve exotique* (*Exotic Eve*) 1890. Oil on board 43 × 25 (17 × $9\frac{7}{8}$). Private Collection

83 *Nirvana. Portrait de Meyer de Haan* 1889. Oil on silk 20 × 29 (8 × 11). Wadsworth Atheneum, Hartford, Ella Gallup Sumner and Mary Catlin Sumner Collection

84 Jacob Meyer de Haan *Farmyard at Le Pouldu* 1889. Oil on canvas 73.5 × 93 (29 × $36\frac{5}{8}$). Rijksmuseum Kröller-Müller, Otterlo

85 *Rentrée des vaches à Pont-Aven* 1889? Pencil on paper 13 × 25.5 ($5\frac{1}{8}$ × 10). Private Collection. Photo courtesy Sotheby's, London

86 *Ramasseuses de varech* (*Seaweed Gatherers*) 1889. Oil on canvas 87.5 × 123 ($34\frac{1}{2}$ × $48\frac{3}{4}$). Folkwang Museum, Essen

87 *Moisson en Bretagne* (*Harvesting in Brittany*) 1889. Oil on canvas 92 × 73 ($36\frac{1}{4}$ × $28\frac{3}{4}$). Courtauld Institute Galleries, London

88 *Soyez amoureuses et vous serez heureuses* (*Be in Love and You Will be Happy*) 1889. Carved, polished and polychromed linden wood 119.7 × 96.8 ($47\frac{1}{8}$ × $38\frac{1}{8}$). Courtesy Museum of Fine Arts, Boston, Arthur Tracy Cabot Fund

89 Self-Portrait Jug, 1889. Stoneware h. 19.5 ($7\frac{5}{8}$). Kunstindustrimuseet, Copenhagen

90 *Le Christ jaune* (*The Yellow Christ*) 1889. Oil on canvas 92 × 73 ($36\frac{1}{4}$ × $28\frac{3}{4}$). Albright-Knox Art Gallery, Buffalo, New York, General Purchase Fund

91 Crucifix from the chapel at Le Trémalo, near Pont-Aven. Photo Belinda Thomson

92 Study for *Le Christ jaune* 1889. Pencil on paper. Private Collection

93 Yann D'Argent *Le Calvaire de Quillinen près de Quimper* (*The Calvary of Quillinen, near Quimper*) 1893. Oil on canvas 98 × 56 ($38\frac{1}{2}$ × 22). Musée des Beaux-Arts, Quimper

94 Deposition from the calvary at Nizon, near Pont-Aven. Photo Belinda Thomson

95 *Le Christ vert. Le Calvaire Breton* (*The Green Christ. Breton Calvary*) 1889. Oil on canvas 92 × 73 ($36\frac{1}{4}$ × $28\frac{3}{4}$). Musées Royaux des Beaux-Arts de Belgique, Brussels

96 *Le Christ au Jardin des Olives* (*Christ in the Garden of Olives*) 1889. Oil on canvas 73 × 92 ($28\frac{3}{4}$ × $36\frac{1}{4}$). Norton Gallery and School of Art, West Palm Beach, Florida

97 Design for the decoration of a bookcase, 1888. Pen and indian ink and watercolour 26 × 19 ($10\frac{1}{4}$ × $7\frac{1}{2}$). Private Collection. Photo courtesy Sotheby's, London

98 Breton *lit clos* (box bed). Musée de Bretagne, Rennes

99 Letter to Vincent Van Gogh, November 1889, with sketches of *Soyez amoureuses* and *Le Christ au Jardin des Olives*. Collection National Museum Vincent Van Gogh, Amsterdam

100 *Bonjour M Gauguin* (*Good Day, M. Gauguin*) 1889. Oil on canvas 113 × 92 ($44\frac{1}{2}$ × $36\frac{1}{4}$). Private Collection, Los Angeles

101 *Portrait charge de Gauguin* (*Caricature Self-Portrait*) 1889. Oil on wood 79.2 × 51.3 ($31\frac{1}{4}$ × $20\frac{1}{4}$). National Gallery of Art, Washington. Chester Dale Collection

102 Marc-Antoine Verdier *Le Christ couronné d'épines. Portrait d'Alfred Bruyas* (*Christ Crowned with Thorns. Portrait of Alfred Bruyas*) *c.* 1850. Oil on canvas 55 × 65 ($21\frac{5}{8}$ × $25\frac{1}{2}$). Musée Fabre, Montpellier

103 Interior of the dining room at the inn of Marie Henry at Le Pouldu, with murals by Gauguin and Meyer de Haan

104 *Portrait de femme à la nature morte de Cézanne* (*Portrait of a woman with Cézanne Still-Life*) 1890. Oil on canvas 65 × 55 ($25\frac{5}{8}$ × $21\frac{5}{8}$). Courtesy of the Art Institute of Chicago, Joseph Winterbotham Collection

105 *La Perte de pucelage* (*The Loss of Virginity*) 1890. Oil on canvas 90 × 130 ($35\frac{1}{2}$ × $51\frac{1}{4}$). The Chrysler Museum, Norfolk, Virginia, Gift of Walter P. Chrysler, Jr.

106 Paul Cézanne *Nature morte, compotier, verre et pommes* (*Still-Life, Fruit Dish, Glass and Apples*) *c.* 1880. Oil on canvas 49 × 55 ($19\frac{1}{4}$ × $21\frac{1}{2}$). Private Collection

107 *Olympia (copie d'après Manet)* (*Copy of Manet's 'Olympia'*) 1891. Oil on canvas 89 × 130 (35 × $51\frac{1}{4}$). Private Collection

108 *La Moisson au bord de la mer* (*Harvest by the Sea*) 1890. Oil on canvas 73 × 92 ($28\frac{3}{4}$ × $36\frac{1}{4}$). Tate Gallery, London

109 Study for *La Perte de pucelage* 1890–1. Charcoal on paper 31.3 × 32.5 ($12\frac{3}{8}$ × $12\frac{3}{4}$). Chicago, Mr and Mrs Leigh B. Block Collection

110 *Portrait de Stéphane Mallarmé* 1891. Etching on brown paper 18.2 × 14.3 ($7\frac{1}{8}$ × $5\frac{5}{8}$). Courtesy of the Art Institute of Chicago, the Albert H. Wolf Memorial Collection

111 Paul Gauguin photographed with his children Emile and Aline in 1891 in Copenhagen

112 *E Haere oe i hia? (Where are you going?)* 1892. Oil on canvas 96 × 69 ($37\frac{3}{4}$ × $27\frac{1}{8}$). Staatsgalerie, Stuttgart
113 View of Papeete, Tahiti, *c.* 1890. Photo Musée de l'Homme, Paris
114 *Montagnes Tahitiennes (Tahitian Landscape)* 1891. Oil on canvas 68 × 92 ($26\frac{3}{4}$ × $36\frac{3}{8}$). The Minneapolis Institute of Arts, Julius C. Eliel Memorial Fund
115 *Suzanne Bambridge* 1891. Oil on canvas 70 × 50 ($27\frac{1}{2}$ × $19\frac{5}{8}$). Musées Royaux des Beaux-Arts de Belgique, Brussels
116 *Le Repas (The Meal)* 1891. Oil on canvas 73 × 92 ($28\frac{3}{4}$ × $36\frac{1}{4}$). Musée d'Orsay, Paris. Photo Réunion des musées nationaux
117 *Vahine no te tiare (Woman with a flower)* 1891. Oil on canvas 70.5 × 46.5 ($27\frac{3}{4}$ × $18\frac{1}{4}$). Ny Carlsberg Glyptotek, Copenhagen
118 *Te faaturuma (Brooding Woman)* 1891. Oil on canvas 92 × 68 ($36\frac{1}{4}$ × $26\frac{3}{4}$). Worcester Art Museum, Worcester, Massachusetts
119 *Te poipoi (Morning Ablutions)* 1892. Oil on canvas 68 × 92 ($26\frac{3}{4}$ × $36\frac{1}{4}$). Collection of the late Joan Whitney Payson
120 *Deux femmes sur la plage (Two Women on the Beach)* 1891. Oil on canvas 69 × 90 ($27\frac{1}{8}$ × $35\frac{1}{2}$). Musée d'Orsay, Paris. Photo Réunion des musées nationaux
121 *Ta Matete (We shall not go to Market Today)* 1892. Oil on canvas 73 × 91.5 ($28\frac{3}{4}$ × $36\frac{1}{4}$). Kunstmuseum, Basel
122 *Ia Orana Maria (Hail Mary)* 1891. Oil on canvas 113.7 × 87.7 ($44\frac{3}{4}$ × $34\frac{1}{2}$). The Metropolitan Museum of Art, New York, Bequest of Sam A. Lewisohn
123 *Une fille* (study for *Parau na te varua ino*) 1892? Charcoal and pastel with watercolour 77 × 35.5 ($30\frac{1}{4}$ × 14). Kupferstichkabinett, Basel
124 *Parau na te varua ino (Words of the Devil)* 1892. Oil on canvas 91.7 × 68.5 ($36\frac{1}{8}$ × 27). National Gallery of Art, Washington, Gift Of the W. Averell Harriman Foundation in memory of Maria N. Harriman
125 Odilon Redon *La Mort, mon ironie dépasse toutes les autres (Death, My Irony Surpasses All Others)* 1888. Lithograph 26.2 × 19.7 ($10\frac{1}{4}$ × $7\frac{3}{4}$). Bibliothèque Nationale, Paris
126 *La Montagne sacrée (The Sacred Mountain)* 1892. Study for *Parahi te marae*. Watercolour over graphite 18.5 × 22.9 ($7\frac{1}{4}$ × 9). Courtesy of the Harvard University Art Museums (Fogg Art Museum), Bequest – Marian Harris Phinney
127 *Buddha's meeting with an ajiwaka monk*, relief from the Temple of Borobudur, Java
128 *Ia Orana Maria (Hail Mary)*. Woodcut pasted into the Louvre manuscript of *Noa Noa*. Musée du Louvre, Paris, Cabinet des Dessins. Photo Réunion des musées nationaux
129 Luc-Olivier Merson *Je vous salue, Marie (Hail Mary) c.* 1885. Oil on canvas 81.3 × 59.7 (32 × $23\frac{1}{2}$). The High Museum of Art, Atlanta, Gift of the Piedmont Driving Club
130 Jules Bastien-Lepage *Jeanne écoutant les voix (Joan of Arc)* 1879. Oil on canvas 254 × 279.4 (100 × 110). The Metropolitan Museum of Art, Gift of Erwin Davis, 1889
131 *Te tamari no atua (The Birth of Christ)* 1896. Oil on canvas 96 × 126 ($37\frac{3}{4}$ × $50\frac{3}{8}$). Neue Pinakothek, Munich
132 *Aha oe feii? (What, are you jealous?)* 1892. Oil on canvas 68 × 92 ($26\frac{3}{4}$ × $36\frac{1}{4}$). Pushkin Museum, Moscow
133 Study for *Nafea faa ipoipo* 1892. Pencil, charcoal and pastel, squared up 55.2 × 47.9 ($21\frac{3}{4}$ × $18\frac{7}{8}$). Courtesy of the Art Institute of Chicago, Gift of Tiffany and Mary Blake
134 *Nafea faa ipoipo? (When will you marry?)* 1892. Oil on conavas 105 × 77 ($41\frac{3}{8}$ × $30\frac{1}{4}$). Collection Rudolf Staechelin, Basel
135 *L'Homme à la hâche (Man with an Axe)* 1891. Oil on canvas 92 × 70 ($36\frac{1}{4}$ × $27\frac{1}{2}$). Private Collection Courtesy Ellen Melas Kyriazi
136 Pierre-Paul Prudhon *Joseph et la femme de Potiphar (Joseph and Potiphar's Wife) c.* 1820. Reproduced in Ch. Clement, *Prud'hon, sa vie, ses œuvres et sa correspondance* 1872. Photo Bibliothèque Nationale, Paris
137 *Joseph et la femme de Potiphar (Joseph and Potiphar's Wife)* 1894. Oil on canvas 89 × 116 (35 × $45\frac{5}{8}$). Present whereabouts unknown
138 *Vahine no te vi (Woman with a mango)* 1892. Oil on canvas 72.7 × 44.5 ($28\frac{5}{8}$ × $17\frac{1}{2}$). The Baltimore Museum of Art: The Cone Collection, formed by Dr Claribel Cone and Miss Etta Cone of Baltimore, Maryland
139 Egyptian fresco from a tomb at Thebes of the XVIIIth dynasty. British Museum, London
140 *Te nave nave fenua (Delicious Land)* 1892. Oil on canvas 91 × 72 ($35\frac{5}{8}$ × $28\frac{3}{8}$). Ohara Museum of Art, Kurashiki
141 Eugène Carrière *Portrait de Paul Gauguin* 1891. Oil on canvas 54.6 × 65.4 ($21\frac{1}{2}$ × $25\frac{3}{4}$). Yale University Art Gallery, Bequest of Fred T. Murphy, B.A. 1897
142 *Merahi metua no Teha'amana (The Ancestors of Teha'amana)* 1893. Oil on canvas 75 × 53 ($29\frac{1}{2}$ × $20\frac{3}{4}$). Courtesy of the Art Institute of Chicago, Charles Deering McCormick Collection
143 *Vairaoumati tei oa (Her Name is Vairaoumati)* 1892. Oil on canvas 91 × 68 ($35\frac{3}{4}$ × $26\frac{3}{4}$). Hermitage Museum, Leningrad
144 Letter to Sérusier, 25 March 1892, with sketch of *Vairaoumati*. Reproduced in P. Sérusier, *A.B.C. de la peinture* 1950
145 *Nave nave moe (Delicious Water)* 1894. Oil on canvas 73 × 98 ($28\frac{3}{4}$ × $38\frac{5}{8}$). Hermitage Museum, Leningrad
146 *Idole à la perle (Idol with a Pearl)* 1892–3. Tamanu wood, stained and gilded h. 25 ($9\frac{7}{8}$). Musée d'Orsay, Paris. Photo Réunion des musées nationaux
147 Gauguin and friends, including Paul Sérusier and Anna la Javanaise, in his studio at 6 rue Vercingétorix, 1894–5
148 *Pape moe (Mysterious Water)* 1893. Oil on canvas 99 × 75 (39 × $29\frac{5}{8}$). Bührle Collection, Zürich
149 *Manau tupapau (The Spirit of the Dead Keeps Watch)* 1892. Oil on canvas 73 × 92 ($28\frac{3}{4}$ × $36\frac{1}{4}$). Albright-Knox Art Gallery, Buffalo, New York, A. Conger Goodyear Collection
150 *Fatata te miti (Near the Sea)* 1892. Oil on canvas 67.9 × 91.5 ($26\frac{3}{4}$ × 36). National Gallery of Art, Washington, Chester Dale Collection
151 *Otahi (Alone)* 1893. Oil on canvas 50 × 73 ($19\frac{1}{2}$ × $28\frac{5}{8}$). Private Collection
152 *Mahana no atua (Day of God)* 1894. Oil on canvas 69.6 × 90.5 ($27\frac{3}{8}$ × $35\frac{5}{8}$). Courtesy of the Art Institute of Chicago, Helen Birch Bartlett Collection

153 *Hina Tefatou* (*The Moon and the Earth*) 1893. Oil on canvas 112 × 62 (44⅛ × 24⅜). Museum of Modern Art, New York. Lillie P. Bliss Collection

154 Georges Manzana Pissarro *Portrait de Gauguin en pied* (*Standing Portrait of Gauguin*) c. 1906. Gouache heightened with gilded bronze 45 × 32 (17¾ × 12⅝). Private Collection

155 Page 57 from the Louvre manuscript of *Noa Noa*, with woodcut of Hina and Tefatou from *Te Atua*, photograph of Tahitian girl and a watercolour. Musée du Louvre, Paris, Cabinet des Dessins. Photo Réunion des musées nationaux

156 *Aita Tamari Vahine Judith Te Parari* (*Anna the Javanese*) 1893–4. Oil on canvas 116 × 81.5 (45¾ × 32). Private Collection

157 *Noa Noa* (*Very Fragrant*) 1894. Woodcut 35.4 × 20.5 (14 × 8). Courtesy of the Art Institute of Chicago, Buckingham Fund

158, 159 Pages 67 and 75 from the Louvre manuscript of *Noa Noa*, with woodcuts and watercolours. Musée du Louvre, Paris, Cabinet des Dessins. Photo Réunion des musées nationaux

160 *D'Où venons-nous? Que sommes-nous? Où allons-nous?* (*Where Are We From? What Are We? Where Are We Going?*) 1897. Oil on canvas 139.1 × 374.6 (54¾ × 147½). Courtesy Museum of Fine Arts, Boston, Tompkins Collection

161 *L'Angélus* (*The Angelus*) 1894. Monotype on paper with watercolour additions 27.4 × 30.5 (10¾ × 12). The Josefowitz Collection

162 *Faa Iheihe* (*Tahitian Pastoral*) 1898. Oil on canvas 54 × 169 (21½ × 66½). Tate Gallery, London

163 *Nevermore, O Tahiti* 1897. Oil on canvas 60 × 116 (23⅝ × 45¾). Courtauld Institute Galleries, London (Courtauld Collection)

164 *Oviri* 1894–5. Stoneware, glazed in parts, painted h. 74 (29⅛). Musée d'Orsay, Paris. Photo courtesy of the Arts Council of Great Britain

165 The new room in the South Wing of the Museum at Auckland, New Zealand, opened in 1892, showing carved panels used in decorating Maori dwellings

166 Cylinder with Christ on the Cross, 1896. Bronze cast of wooden original h. 50 (19⅝). Private Collection. Photo courtesy Sotheby's London

167 Menhir de Pleuven, Pleumeur-Bodou, Côtes du Nord. Photo Musée de Bretagne, Rennes

168 *Te arii vahine* (*Woman with Mangos*) 1896. Oil on canvas 97 × 128 (38¼ × 51⅛). Hermitage Museum, Leningrad

169 Lucas Cranach the Elder *Nymphe endormie* (*Sleeping Nymph*) 1537. Oil on wood 48.5 × 74.2 (19⅞ × 29¼). Musée des Beaux-Arts de Besançon

170 *Te Rerioa* (*The Dream*) 1897. Oil on canvas 95 × 132 (37⅜ × 52). Courtauld Institute Galleries, London (Courtauld Collection)

171 Two Tahitian Heads c. 1902. Traced monotype 32.1 × 51 (12⅝ × 20⅛) British Museum, London

172 First page of a letter to Daniel de Monfreid, February 1898, with sketch of *D'Où venons-nous?*. Private Collection

173 Squared up study of *D'Où venons-nous?* 1889? Watercolour on pasted-up tracing paper 20.5 × 37.5 (8⅛ × 14¾). Musée des Arts Africains et Océaniens, Paris

174 Pierre Puvis de Chavannes *Inter Artes et Naturam* (*Amid the Arts and Nature*) 1890. 295 × 830 (116 × 327). Musée des Beaux-Arts, Rouen

175 Paul Sérusier *Pont-Aven Triptych* 1892–3. Oil on canvas 73 × 133 (28¾ × 52⅜). Private Collection

176 Paul Signac *Au Temps d'Harmonie* (*In the Age of Harmony*) 1894–5. Oil on canvas 300 × 400 (118 × 157½). Mairie de Montreuil, Paris. Photo Suzanne Bosman

177 *Nos Coloniaux* (*Our Colonialists*) c. 1900. Pen and indian ink 47.5 × 63.5 (18¾ × 25). Private Collection. Photo courtesy Sotheby's, London

178 *Le Sourire* c. 1899–1900. Woodcut 10.3 × 18.3 (4⅛ × 7¼). Pasted into the Louvre manuscript of *Noa Noa*. Musée du Louvre, Paris, Cabinet des Dessins. Photo Réunion des musées nationaux

179 *Nature morte avec 'L'Espérance' de Puvis* (*Still-Life with Puvis' 'Hope'*) 1901. Oil on canvas 65 × 77 (25⅝ × 30¼). From the collection of Mrs Joanne Toor Cummings, New York

180 *Contes barbares* (*Barbarous Tales*) 1902. Oil on canvas 130 × 89 (51⅛ × 35). Folkwang Museum, Essen

181 *Cavaliers sur la plage* (*Horsemen on the Beach*) 1902. Oil on canvas 66 × 76 (26 × 35). Folkwang Museum, Essen

182 *Femme Tahitienne accroupie vue de dos* (*Crouching Tahitian woman seen from the back*) 1901–2. Gouache monotype 53.3 × 28.3 (21 × 11⅛). Eugene V. Thaw Collection

Index